THE BOOK OF
Norse Magic

THE BOOK OF
Norse *Magic*

Charms, incantations, and spells harnessing the power of runes, ancient gods and goddesses, and more

Cerridwen Greenleaf

CICO BOOKS

LONDON NEW YORK

Published in 2022 by CICO Books
An imprint of Ryland Peters & Small Ltd

20–21 Jockey's Fields   341 E 116th St
London WC1R 4BW   New York, NY 10029

www.rylandpeters.com

10 9 8 7 6 5 4 3 2 1

A CIP catalog record for this book is available from the
Library of Congress and the British Library.

ISBN: 978-1-80065-124-1

Printed in China

Editor: Caroline West
Illustrator: Nina Hunter
Crystal photographer: Roy Palmer

Commissioning editor: Kristine Pidkameny
Senior commissioning editor: Carmel Edmonds
Senior designer: Emily Breen
Art director: Sally Powell
Creative director: Leslie Harrington
Head of production: Patricia Harrington
Publishing manager: Penny Craig
Publisher: Cindy Richards

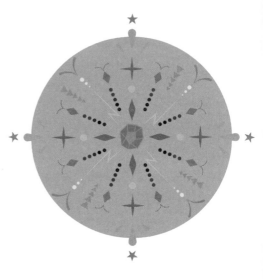

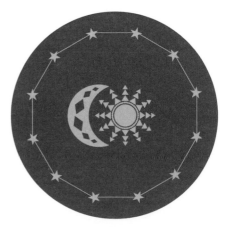

Contents

INTRODUCTION:
Ancient Magic for the Modern World

What is Norse magic? Put simply, it is magic that's deeply rooted in the old ways and helps you forge a personal path which honors the ancient while harnessing the power of the past to enhance today's daily living. It is a singular craft that champions and encourages individualism, while retaining an all-important connection to a spiritual tribe.

My intention for this book is that it should be your all-inclusive guide to the art of magic for modern-day living. It contains information on the history of magic, as well as its various practices, and marks a next step beyond Wicca (the pagan religion that practices witchcraft) for beginners. If you are a spiritual adventurer who likes to look beyond the visible realm and explore the ancient, hidden, and mysterious—to discover a marvelous and unexpected world of enchantment—then this is the book is for you. It will help you gain a fuller understanding of what makes this kind of Nordic magic unique and provide you with a stepping-off point for self-exploration and the creation of personalized spells and tribal rituals. The chapters contain rituals, charms, and spells, which range from simple "quickie" spells to more complex enchantments designed to mark very special rites of passage and engender the deepest personal transformation. This is an instruction book for anyone hoping to lead an utterly enchanted and empowered life.

Light and Shadow: Creating Your Nordic Altar

There are many ways in which to nurture your truest nature and soul; perhaps the most obvious is to create a Nordic altar. To do this, you can choose the classic symbols of the north and winter—white, icicles, clear crystals, and so on—but do not limit yourself to these. Such symbols only skim the surface of the possibilities. What about a fossil that is frozen in the amber of time? Perhaps a birch branch with delicate lichen barely clinging to the surface. Think of how a frozen lake glistens with many colors and the mystery that lies beneath the surface, both of which can be represented by an iridescent and glittery chunk of labradorite crystal for your altar. Or, as you take a walk in the darkening days leading up to the Winter Solstice (December 21), collect a fallen leaf, which is a perfect dried emblem of the changing season. In your own backyard, you may see a tiny acorn, tucked into the roots of an old oak tree. Place this on your altar as a symbol of potentiality. As you pass by a yard sale, you spy a piece of beautiful carved ivory, an antique whale-tooth scrimshaw depicting an Inuit ritual, and you instantly know it is perfect for your

sacred space. In the back of your closet, you find a snow globe you prized as a child; it has swirling, snowy flakes inside a perfect sphere. Suddenly, you remember your favorite Hans Christian Andersen fairy tale, The Snow Queen. You place the book on your altar and open to a gorgeously pre-Raphaelite depiction of this royal embodiment of the Winter Soul.

Encouraged and feeling more open and adventurous, you try your hand at art. You paint a triptych for your altar—a hoary sky, the palest of suns struggling to shine, a low-hung harvest moon, all beautiful blues with a sapphire night sky and silver stars. As you think about the heavens above and the firmament in which hang the stars, moon, sun, and all the planets, you are struck by a sense of the sacred. You feel how very special it is to be alive on this planet, perhaps an accident and most definitely a miracle. As you think about it, you can almost feel the swing of the Earth on its axis as it spins around the sun. Now more than ever, you feel so very alive.

DUSK IS DIVINE ALTAR CONSECRATION RITUAL

Once you have collected items for your altar and arranged everything to your liking, now is the time to consecrate the space. You can use a ritual of your own or follow the simple instructions provided here. The best time to perform this ritual is at dusk.

The incense should come from a resinous tree, ideally one that grows in northern lands such as the balsam fir (*Abies balsamea*) or Norway spruce (*Picea abies*). Light the candles and place them on your altar. Now, light the incense and fan it with the feather, as birds are the harbingers of change. As you breathe in the scented smoke, pray aloud:

I welcome positive inside of me,

I know my deepest wish is real and right.

I will my spirit to be free

Under this silver moon in this dark night.

Spirits of the heavens—
bless this space with all due grace.

So mote it be!

Gather Together

Balsam fir incense

1 purple candle

1 white candle

Matches

Single white feather

Chapter 1

RUNES AND DIVINE DIVINATION

Runes were hugely important to the Norse people. Discover how these mystical symbols can offer insight into the future as well as enhance other witchy rituals.

An Introduction to Runes as a Magical Tool

During the Dark Ages, northern Europeans practiced a sort of "primal paganism." The Germanic tribes of northern Europe included the Goths (the Visigoths and Ostrogoths from southern Scandinavia); the Vandals from what is now southern Poland; the Lombards from northwest Germany; the Burgundians, a Scandinavian people from the southern shores of the Baltic Sea; and the Franks who hailed from near the Rhine River in Germany. These tribes (or Goths as they popularly became known) made quite a name for themselves as they moved across Europe, spreading destruction in their wake and even ransacking the mighty Rome. Their violent antics earned them the name "barbarian," which was later replaced by the much more colorful term goth, meaning "uncivilized." Gothic spirituality was informed by a mythology that is best described by the Roman historian Tacitus in *Germany and Its Tribes*: "In their ancient songs, their only way of remembering or recording the past, they celebrate an earth-born god Tuisco, and his son Mannus, as the origin of race, as their founders." Powerful female elders, or "seeresses," passed down this pagan mythology through an oral tradition. Runes, a symbolic system used for signs and omens, were the only form of writing used by these tribes.

I count myself as coming from this Germanic lineage to a great extent, a belief that stems from family lore backed up scientifically by a DNA test I took a couple of years ago. The discovery of my heritage has inspired this aspect of my work. Furthermore, one of the great delights of my life in recent years was discovering from my DNA test that I have a West African great-great-grandparent and a Native American great-great-grandparent. I count myself fortunate indeed to have these many connections in my makeup, but I wish to emphasize that Norse magic is for absolutely everyone! I feel it is also important to point out that Norse magic is, of course, white magic in that it is positive and not negative, or black, magic.

I feel very connected to this ancestry and to my forebears, sensing in particular the power of the women who came before me. I have also noticed that as I grow older, my psychic ability becomes stronger. I can often "feel" what people are thinking. I suddenly just know things and believe that my work with tools of divination has enhanced this latent ability in me and can also do the same for you. I have worked with runes since high school and was greatly inspired to build upon that foundation once I saw the scientific evidence of my Nordic roots.

Runes and the Wisdom of the Divine

Runes are the letters that make up the runic alphabet—an ancient writing system that was used by various Germanic peoples, from Sweden to Germany to the British Isles, to transcribe their languages. The earliest known inscriptions come from around 150 CE and the same runes are still being used today for many forms of divination and magic. The straight, angular strokes that make up the characters made them ideal for cutting into slabs of wood along the grain. There were also no horizontal strokes, which meant that carving the runes would not cause the wood to split.

Runes are most often associated with the Vikings, and the word itself is derived from the Common Germanic word *runo*, meaning "letter, mystery, or secret." Each rune represented a speech sound, but was also thought to have its own distinct, alternate meanings, which were linked to the cultural and religious beliefs of the Germanic peoples.

DISCOVER THE RUNES THAT ARE RIGHT FOR YOU

Long ago, I chose the lovely and very sturdy Anglo-Saxon Futhark as the runes I work with. It was based on how they looked to me and I could see the ancient lineage in how the runes were shaped. I have never looked back and my affection for them grows over time. There are other choices so do study the runes and spend time with them, drawing and contemplating them. It won't be long before you make your choice of the runes that resonates the most for you to employ in your magical workings. The various rune sets include:

- Elder Futhark (2nd to 8th centuries)
- Anglo-Saxon runes (5th to 11th centuries)
- "Marcomannic runes" (8th to 9th centuries)
- Younger Futhark (9th to 11th centuries)
- Medieval runes (12th to 15th centuries)
- 3.6 Dalecarlian runes (16th to 19th centuries)

Rune Meanings

Ansuz (A): Sign/Message

This rune is primarily associated with communication. It can be a sign of inspiration or divine wisdom, truth-seeking, advice, and visions. If this rune is reversed, that can mean you are not being open-minded, or point to difficulties in communication.

Berkana (B): Birch Goddess

Berkana represents fertility and the growth of new relationships and projects, as well as spiritual and emotional growth, regeneration, family, nurturing, and the flexibility of the birch tree. Its reversed meaning can be a sign of anxiety or familial issues.

Dagaz (D): Day

Dagaz symbolizes innovation. It suggests clarity and a new awakening. It is a hopeful symbol that connotes change, beginnings, and contentment, and cannot be reversed.

Ehwaz (E): Horse

This rune is symbolic of movement. As the rune of the horse, Ehwaz is related to transportation, moving on from past hurts, positive changes, teamwork, consistent progress, and devotion. When reversed, it may be indicative of a longing for change, restlessness, or a lack of trust.

Eihwaz (EI): Yew

The rune of the yew is related to spiritual transformation, the passing of the old to make way for the new, endurance, trustworthiness, and intention. It has no reverse.

Fehu (F): Wealth / Cattle

Fehu represents possessions, either earned or won wealth, great prosperity, luck, and happiness. The reversed rune can be a sign of loss related to money, personal belongings, or even self-esteem or emotional burnout. It may also indicate greed.

Gebo (G): Gift

This rune represents exchanges, gift-giving, blessings, relationships, talents, balance, and generosity. This is a very positive rune, and it has no reverse. It may, however, be in opposition, in which case it can mean excessive self-sacrifice, loneliness, greed, or obligation.

Hagalaz (H): Hail

Just like natural disaster, Hagalaz symbolizes sudden and often irreversible change that is out of one's control. It has the potential for disruption and destruction, but it is also a sign of lessons learned through hardship. Hagalaz does not have a reverse.

Isa (I): Ice

This rune is related to a trial or challenge and exasperation, and is often symbolic of a stalemate or delay. It indicates a time to wait and find perspective in the stillness. Isa cannot be reversed.

Jera (J): Harvest

Jera is indicative of reaping the fruits of one's labors, a period of immense joy, and cycles of life, gratitude, and abundance. It is another rune that has no reverse.

Kenaz (K): Illumination

The rune Kenaz is literally translated as a "torch made of pine wood" and symbolizes fire and light. It is connected to enlightenment, knowledge, creativity, and new energies. It is also a rune of transformation. Reversed, its meaning is often related to creative blocks, blindness to truth, false hope, and the destructive power of unattended fire.

Laguz (L): Water / Lake

Laguz represents the element of water, and as such it is strongly associated with emotions and dreamwork. It is a sign of healing, respite, imagination, and psychic abilities. It can be taken as a hint to let go of old behaviors and ideas that are harmful or no longer serving you. Reversed, this rune is associated with confusion and fear, poor decisions, or a feeling of being overwhelmed.

Mannaz (M): Man

This rune symbolizes humankind and the self. It is related to your identity and the opinions you have of others, and vice versa. It represents relationships, morality, and collaboration. Reversed, it can be a sign of delusion, loneliness, seclusion, and manipulation.

Nauthiz (N): Need

Nauthiz is a rune that indicates we need something or that something is missing in our lives. It is also related to restraint, patience, survival, persistence, affliction, and hardship that overwhelms. It can be a harsh rune and has no reverse. Positive and negative meanings in this rune are inextricably connected.

Ingwaz (NG): God of Fertility

This rune symbolizes fertility, sexuality, family and the home, fulfillment, practicality, restfulness, and peace of mind. This rune has no reverse.

Othala (O): Inheritance

Othala is indicative of one's homeland, tradition, heritage, heirlooms, destiny, and ancestral power. It can be related to your family ties and the strength of your relationships. When reversed, it can mean poverty, neglectfulness, obsession with the material, and bad luck.

Perthro (P): Unknown Meaning

The precise meaning of this rune is unknown. However, it is associated with destiny, fortune, matters of the future, change, and secrets. The reversed meaning can be hopelessness, inaction, and unsuccessful risk-taking.

Raidho (R): Journey

Raidho is a rune connected to travel, change, cycles, and open-mindedness. Reversed, it is a sign of inflexibility, close-mindedness, stagnation, and a lack of perspective.

Sowilō (S): Sun

This rune is symbolic of the power of the sun, happiness, positive growth, good luck, passion, and health. There is no reverse of Sowilō.

Tiwaz (T): Justice

This rune is representative of Tyr, the Norse god of treaty, law, and justice (see page 42). It symbolizes victory, authority, confidence, honor, and good judgment, and it also indicates the leadership, honor, self-assurance, and tenacity of a warrior. Reversed, it can mean you are struggling with blocks, a loss of vigor, failure, or some form of disparity.

Thurisaz (TH): Giant

Thurisaz indicates power, struggle, force, and sudden change. It has cathartic associations and can have a cleansing, purgative meaning for you. Reversed, this rune can be a sign of danger, frustration, treachery, or an inability to defend yourself.

Uruz (U): Wild Ox

The ox rune is a symbol of strength, confidence, hard work and dedication, health, and power. Reversed, it symbolizes weakness, aggression, illness, or loss of motivation.

Wunjo (W): Joy

This is the rune of reward, victory, prosperity, pleasure, security, happiness, and harmony. Its reverse is related to sadness and dismay or loss.

Algiz (Z): Elk

Algiz is a symbol of shielding. It indicates protection from evil, defense, and guardianship. Its reversed meaning warns of a potential danger hidden in your path.

Odin (Unknown): Blank

Odin's rune is left blank, symbolizing one's unknowable fate—the mysteries and secrets that the future holds. In a reading, it could be a sign that there are aspects of your question which cannot be answered. It can also replace one of your pieces if it is lost. (For more on the Norse god Odin, see page 38.)

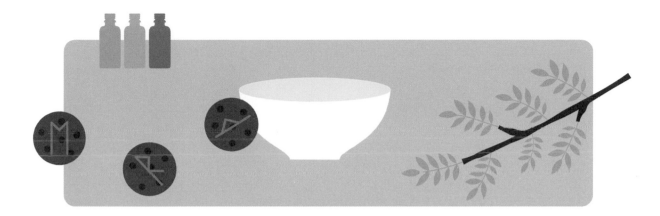

RUNE BLESSING BOWL RITE

Keeping your runes in a bowl on an altar (see page 20) is helpful, since this makes them portable if you need to do readings elsewhere.

A rich part of the runic tradition was that the runes were often carved out of wood, so I like to keep mine in a medium-sized wooden bowl with a thick rim. I also like to put the runes in a green velvet bag if I need to take them to a ceremony or a reading at another venue. The green of the bag represents the trees that provided the wood out of which the runes were carved. Note that it is important to cleanse the energy of the rune stones after every reading. Smudging with sage will certainly work (see page 21), but I prefer to use Palo Santo (wood from *Bursera graveolens*), which means "holy tree" in Spanish. I also like to rub one drop of Palo Santo essential oil on the rim of the wooden bowl to cleanse the energy after readings. As I do so, I intone the following:

These runes are a tool I use for good.

Everything will be known, as it should.

Clarity and understanding in all will come through.

Sacred energy is in flow; it is real and true.

And so it is.

RIME AND RITUAL: CREATING YOUR RUNIC ALTAR

Gather Together

Black fabric square and white fabric square, to use as your altar cloth

Table or shelf to designate as the runic altar

Set of runes in a beautiful bowl

Sage bundle for smudging

Matches

Fireproof dish or abalone shell

2 black candles

2 white candles

Mirror to place under the rune bowl

The first thing you need to do to embrace and further develop your psychism and ability to divine is to create a dedicated space for this. Your altar can be a low table or even a shelf.

To begin, lay the two fabric squares on the table or shelf. As a centerpiece, place a set of runes in a beautiful bowl on the altar. First, purify the space with the smoke from a lit sage bundle. This ritual is called "smudging" and is an essential part of witchcraft. You can use wild sage or purchase it in any herb store. Once you have smudged the space, place the black and white candles in each of the four corners. Light the candles. Now pick up the rune bowl with your left hand and the mirror with your right hand. Kneel before your newly created altar, and say:

I light the fire of prophecy, the heat of heart and the flame of truth.

Brightest blessing, Great Seer Goddess bring.

The spirit of knowledge will surely sing.

As the fates do dance, I welcome the chance for visions of the future and all things to come.

So mote it be.

Place the mirror under your bowl of runes and pull out a rune to receive your reading for the day. I pick one rune every morning to provide a daily touchstone and insight into my future for the day and beyond.

SMUDGING

Sometimes we need to cleanse energy from somewhere, whether it's so that we can perform spellwork or rituals, or simply to clear blocks to happiness from our homes. This can be done by burning certain herbs—the smoke clears the negative energy, allowing positive energy to flow again. Sage leaves are excellent for this, but you can also use juniper (see page 71), among others. You can make a smudge stick by binding the herb leaves with rope so that you can transport the smoke around your house. Keep your smudging materials on your altar so you have them to hand. You will also need a fireproof container to carry underneath the smudge stick and leave it to burn in.

The Ancient Art of Rune Casting

Modern practitioners of witchcraft have adapted what we know of this ancient runic language and its traditional magical uses for their own form of divinatory arts. Runes are a splendid tool to help you foretell and interpret the direction your future is going in. They can guide you to an understanding of the likely consequences of your current actions before they come to pass, giving you the opportunity to alter your trajectory and take a different path.

I suggest you approach rune casting by asking a question that is both precise and open-ended. Take into account your current environment and the situations you are involved in when you decide on your question. You will need to dip into your spiritual side and trust in your intuition to give you the answers you seek.

To begin, find a quiet place to conduct your reading. It should be somewhere peaceful, where you are not likely to be interrupted, and you should be facing north. You will need a rune set, which you can either purchase or make yourself (see pages 24–25). Once you have found a place to sit, place an altar cloth in front of you on which to cast the runes. Form the question in your mind as you sit and wait until you are firmly set on your question. Once you are confident, you can begin casting. Below are a few suggestions for how to do this.

Simple Rune Casting

An easy method is to cast your entire bag of runes onto the altar cloth. Interpret the runes by following the meaning of the sides that are facing upright. The connotation of rune stones that fall so they are facing upside down, or reversed, is negative, but does not necessarily indicate that the meaning of the rune is its opposite. Alternatively, for a casting method suitable for beginners, disregard those stones and focus only on those that are facing upright.

7 Rune Casting

For this divination technique, you will select seven runes from your bag at random. Lay the first six runes out in a row in front of you, then place the seventh rune underneath the center of the row. Starting at the left of the row, the first two

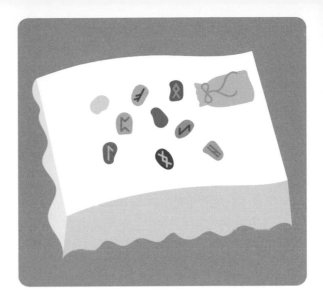

runes are related to the issue at hand. The third and fourth runes, on the other hand, symbolize some variables that led to the current situation. The fifth and sixth runes contain advice for how to deal with your situation. The seventh rune is the conclusion you are headed toward, which you must interpret in light of the previous six runes.

9 Rune Casting

Nine is a significant number in Norse paganism since there are nine worlds supported by Yggdrasil, the World Tree (see page 60), in Norse cosmology. This method of casting involves randomly selecting nine runes from your bag. Choose the nine runes and concentrate on the question you decided on while holding them between your palms, then cast them onto your altar cloth. Start by reading the runes that land face up. Those that land in the center of the cloth will be the most important and relevant runes.

Next, read the rune stones that were scattered facing down. These stones will be symbolic of external influences and can indicate a potential conclusion to the situation you are asking about.

MOONSTONE RUNE STONES

Moonstone is reputed to be the most powerful crystal for making rune stones, which are tools used for a specialized form of divination. Runes, or letters from a language used by early Nordic peoples, are carved into the stones and said to hone and intensify the intuition of the reader divining the future from them. You, too, can use a bag of lustrous and mysterious moonstones to connect with your powers of perception. It is easier to buy a set of moonstone rune stones than it is to carve the symbols into the stones yourself, but I recommend you try to do this since hand-carved symbols connect to the divine quickly and potently. While some people like to throw the I Ching or read their horoscopes with a morning coffee, you can pull a rune and contemplate its meaning for your day. (Find out more about moonstones on page 87.)

Witchcraft: How to Create Your Own Set of Runes

Although there are many places where you can purchase rune sets to begin your rune casting journey, an even better way to start is by creating your own! Handcrafted runes are both easy and affordable to make, and being the result of your own handiwork, they'll be imbued with your unique energy, which will give you a deeper connection to them.

The first stage when creating your rune set is to decide which materials you are going to use. The best sets are made from all-natural materials:

Stones

It is quite common to use smooth stones or pebbles for rune casting. I recommend retrieving small, flat stones from Mother Nature herself by traversing the woods to a stream or river, or perhaps visiting a local beach. You will likely want them to be small enough that you can hold them all cupped in your palms at once. Your options are then to carve them (which can take a significant amount of time) or to paint the runes on the surface.

Wood

This is another excellent choice of material for creating a set of runes. I recommend you use wood from an ash tree, as this is sacred in Norse mythology. Other trees will work as well, however, so use whichever wood feels right for you. You could also create your runes from the branch of a live tree that grows fruit. If you do take from a living tree, be sure to ask it to grant you permission first and water it as a token of your gratitude afterward.

Wood is excellent for carving because it is much easier to work with than stone. You can sculpt out the letters with knives made for carving, or use a heated pyrography tool, both of which make for a more permanent option. Alternatively, just as with a stone set, you can simply paint the surface of wooden runes. If you are not able to retrieve your own wood from nature, it is quite easy to find and buy slices of wood that will serve your purpose quite nicely.

Clay

This is a wonderful material to use for runes because it is so intuitive—you can simply mold it into the shapes and sizes you require and then use a tool to draw runes on the soft surface. Bear in mind, however, that clay runes are also the most prone to breaking. If clay feels right for you, be sure to bake and seal it properly so the runes will last.

Bones

If you feel that a bone rune set is ideal for your divination practice, always ensure the bones are ethically sourced. It is best if the animal died in a natural manner. Bones can also be quite brittle, so choose sturdy ones that won't snap or chip when you cast them.

Inscribe Your Runes

Once you have the rune materials, you can begin inscribing your pieces. These should all be the same general shape and size for optimal casting. You will need 24 pieces, or if you are including Odin's blank rune, you'll need 25 pieces. Paint or carve each one, and practice saying the names of the runes aloud as you do so. You can set the mood with some music that you find pleasing—anything that will help you to focus your intentions as you work.

Consecrate Your Rune Set

Before using your new rune set, you will need to consecrate it. Wait until you are in a healthy state of mind to do this—you want to be feeling happy and peaceful. It's not advisable to consecrate your runes if you've woken up on the wrong side of bed that morning. Be patient and save this meaningful ritual for when any negative emotions have abated. If you already have your own method of consecration, feel free to follow this, but I have included a simple candle consecration that you can use as well.

Rune Set Consecration with Candles

Begin by meditating and getting yourself into the appropriate headspace for ceremony. Light a candle and direct your attention to the ritual at hand, letting other distracting thoughts drift away. All your newly made runes should be placed to the left of the candle. Shift your focus to each rune in turn, one at a time. Pick up the rune from its resting place on your left and say its name aloud. Use a reference sheet if you wish—it's fine to "cheat" at this stage! This process will also help you get to know each of the runes better. Consider the rune's meaning, then pass it carefully over the flame and set it down on the candle's right side. Once you have completed this process with each rune, your consecration is complete. Make ready for your first casting!

Rune Magic

There is so much more to rune magic than just divination! In fact, casting is just one small part of the realm of rune magic. You can use runes in your everyday life as a dynamic magical tool and not just for rituals and enchantments. As you begin to feel deeply in touch with your runes and gain a deeper understanding of them, you will find yourself using them in all sorts of different situations throughout the day.

Simple Rune Magic for Every Day

To get you started, here are some examples of small, practical ways you can use rune magic each and every day.

For healing: You can draw runes on your body to help reduce the symptoms you are experiencing, including aches and pains, headaches, and more. Laguz is a rune of cleansing, which makes it great for blockages, while Uruz is excellent for all-around healing, giving you strength and steadiness, and Kenaz can be useful for fever. I would not consider healing runes an effective cure, but they are great to supplement other methods of self-care and provide some alleviation for you.

When walking: I love to go on nature walks and observe how the runes speak to me as I observe the world around me. If you keep a clear, open mind, you can discover runes just about anywhere—as shapes in the clouds, in sidewalk cracks, hidden in graffiti if you live in the city, or in the patterns of fallen leaves or the boughs of trees.

On the go: Carry a rune stone with you when you're out and about in the same way that you would a crystal, to receive its energies throughout your day.

When preparing or eating food: A very simple way to incorporate rune magic into your day is by tracing runes in the air while you are preparing food and drink for yourself. You can even draw runes with syrup on your morning pancakes! Try to be intentional about the runes you use, selecting them based on your goals and desires for the day.

SACRED ESSENTIAL OILS

I became a sacred oil enthusiast as a teen. For use with runes, I recommend those that come from tree sap, including amber, myrrh, sandalwood, frankincense, palmarosa, bay laurel, and cinnamon. However, I also consider rose, orange, ylang ylang, and bergamot essential oils to be sacred, among others, because of their plant-based origination and magical properties.

When writing: You can practice rune magic by writing your name in runes, or even by writing out whole sentences, affirmations, and so forth, using the runic alphabet. Writing words with runes means you can imbue them with an additional layer of magical meaning.

When signing your name: When you sign your name, begin or end the signature with one of your favorite runes.

For protection: Runes are an excellent tool for protecting your home. Once you have cleansed your space, use a favorite sacred essential oil (see above) to finger-paint runes over all the doorways, windows, and other places through which energy flows in your home. Some excellent runes to use for protection are Algiz and Thurisaz, but you can use whichever runes you feel best suit your household and the energies you want to encourage.

To begin your day: Start your day with some runic yoga-like exercises called stadha! These stretches involve forming the shapes of the runic alphabet with your body—you can find YouTube videos explaining how to do this or pick up a rune magic handbook to help you get started. Author Eldred Thorsson covers runic stadha in his *Handbook of Rune Magic*. I have even found diagrams of rune yoga poses on Pinterest!

As a daily practice: In the morning, select a rune from your set at random and meditate on the meaning of that rune throughout the day. You can make this a daily practice and mark on your calendar which rune you pulled out each day.

For adornment: You can practice rune magic by incorporating runic jewelry pieces into your everyday wardrobe. There are so many lovely small businesses out there selling rune-inscribed bracelets, earrings, necklaces, and more. If you are the creative type, you can also try making some runic jewelry of your own!

For display: Purchase or create your own rune grid to display on your altar or another place where it will be looked at often. Its sacred geometry can be used to enhance your practice and is quite similar to a crystal grid. You simply need to use your rune set instead of gemstones.

CREATE YOUR OWN WEARABLE RUNE CHARM

This charm is incredibly easy to make and a wonderful way to create and carry magic with you wherever you go.

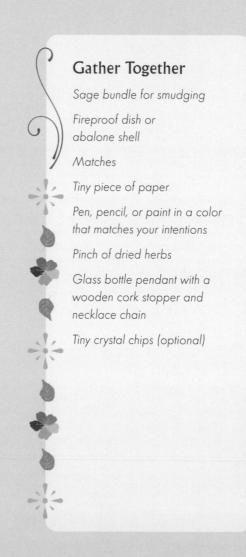

Gather Together

Sage bundle for smudging

Fireproof dish or abalone shell

Matches

Tiny piece of paper

Pen, pencil, or paint in a color that matches your intentions

Pinch of dried herbs

Glass bottle pendant with a wooden cork stopper and necklace chain

Tiny crystal chips (optional)

First, you will need to cleanse all your materials and equipment with the smoke from a lit sage bundle in a ritual known as smudging (see page 21). Once you have a sanctified workspace, write your chosen rune symbol on a very small piece of paper in a color of your choice. Select some herbs from your witchy repertoire, then sprinkle them on the piece of paper and roll this tightly into a tiny scroll. Take care that the herbs don't fall out as you do this. Slide the scroll inside the clean and dry glass bottle, and if you are satisfied, seal with the cork stopper and wear your new necklace. I recommend also adding some crystal chips and other meaningful charms to the bottle, but what you include is up to you!

WITCHY HERBS

Mint sends anxiety and stress away and also calms your stomach.

Thyme helps with letting go and overcoming grief and clears the lungs.

Mullein is a wonderful aid for sleep and simple relaxing.

Sage is renowned for clearing energy, but also tames tension and abets longevity.

Chamomile makes for sweet sleep and helps you attain a meditative state.

Nettle settles digestive ills, aches, and pains, while also enhancing psychic powers.

Oat straw is a brain booster, helps reduce stress, and is a lesser-known love potion!

Echinacea is known for curing colds, but it can also raise mood, immunity, and prosperity.

Lavender is a beloved therapeutic, but also brings mental strength and visionary thinking.

Comfrey is good for bones and skin renewal and will protect both you and your home.

Runes in Ritual

I love to incorporate runes into my rituals. They strengthen the intention of my spells and bring their own unique energy and power. I choose runes based on my intentions for each spell—it is important that you select runes for your rituals with which you have a connection and that are relevant to the kind of spell you are performing. Take the time to get to know the runes and attune yourself to their meanings before you start using them for magic rather than selecting them at random. The time and effort you spend familiarizing yourself with them will pay off splendidly in your spiritual life.

Incorporating Runes into Rituals

Here is a brief list of some other ways to incorporate runes into your rituals:

In artwork: Crafty witches can paint a bind rune on paper or canvas and frame it. Bind runes are unique because they involve "binding" together at least two different runes, then fusing them into one, brand-new symbol. They are commonly used for sigils and talismans. Select runes whose energies complement each other, then hang this rune painting above your altar. A fascinating example of a bind rune is the symbol for Bluetooth, which combines Berkana (see page 14) and Bagall, which is from the Younger Futhark (see page 13) and looks like a star.

For power and protection: Use your fingers to draw runes for protection and power in the air before beginning a ritual or trace them over the surface of your altar.

SIGILS AND TALISMANS

Sigils are symbols you choose to utilize in your magical workings by drawing them or painting them onto a surface, such as a candle, paper, or an altar. A talisman is an object imbued with magical properties. Think of Tolkien's "One Ring" as a great example!

RUNES IN CANDLE MAGIC

Personally, I find that runes lend themselves best to my rituals when I am using candle magic—I inscribe my ritual candles with runes by carving them directly into the wax with a boline (a special, white-handled knife) or the thorn of a rose. You can carve words into your candles using the runic alphabet, or just a single rune to imbue the candle with its distinct personality and intention.

In your sacred space: Take objects that you can find in nature and use them to draw runes in the center of the space you have consecrated for ritual. Some examples of items you might use are leaves, flowers, sticks, pebbles, or even blades of grass!

Into the ground: During your ritual, use a finger or sacred tool to write runes into the very earth beneath you.

For decoration: Emblazon your sacred tools—wands, ritual knives, chalices, or otherwise—with runes.

For self-decoration: Enhance the power of your rituals by painting your skin with runes. You can even combine rune magic with a chakra meditation by, for example, painting the rune of communication, Ansuz, over your Throat chakra, or by using Wunjo for the Heart chakra.

The sky is truly the limit, Dear Reader. Be creative and of an open mind and heart as you continue to explore and uncover the potential of rune magic in your life.

Chapter 2

GODDESSES, GODS, AND LEGENDS

The world of Norse mythology is filled with fascinating stories of ancient magic. Invoke these amazing deities for help in all areas of your life.

Otherworldly Guardians and Guides: Norse Mythology

The northern European tribes had a rich and varied mythology. Long, dark, icy winters dominated the world inhabited by their gods and goddesses. Winter, the longest season for these people, was the time for the rebirthing of the world. For example, the hardy Vikings believed in a "quintessence" in their mythos. Besides the revered four elements so essential to pagan belief—earth, air, fire, and water—they also believed that winter itself had a unique energy, which made it the fifth element. In ancient and medieval philosophy, quintessence was the fifth and highest element after the four elements. It was thought to be the substance of the heavenly bodies and latent in all things. At that time, the entire tradition of the northern tribes held that all life in the world came from Niflheim, a world made entirely of ice. It was a cold, white world of snow and sleet. The counterpart world to the south was Muspelheim—this was hot and fiery, and teeming with volcanoes. The first being ever to set foot in the world was a frost giant called Ymir, who materialized from an enormous block of ice.

Unfortunately for us, the Vikings were too busy surviving to create written records of their tales and mythologies. We do, however, have the vast epic poems that were sung, passed down through generations, and finally written down, the Icelandic Eddas being among them. These poems provide a rich resource to help us understand the Nordic mind. Vikings were great storytellers with an incredible ability to recite hours and hours of story and song from memory. The storytellers were known as *skalds* and were held in high regard by their communities.

A visiting *skald* was an occasion for a fine feast attended by both king and commoners in a great hall, with a roaring fire, roasting meats, and many a jug of mead. Iceland was the last stronghold of the old Viking religion and tales, as it was too distant and remote for most invasions and for Christian military missionaries to visit. Keenly aware of their role as preservationists, the Vikings began recording the Old Norse sagas and songs, and thus we have the Eddas. The first edda, the Prose Edda, was written down in the early 13th century, and the second, the Poetic Edda, in the late 13th century. These collections are the single most important original text for understanding the true nature and mindset of the Norse, the original Gothic pagans. As modern dark Wiccans, we are continuing the legacy and mythology of the Old Norse oral tradition with our stories, ceremonies, and writings.

A Guide to Other Realms

We regularly tap into the wisdom and lore of Norse deities since the days of the week are almost entirely named after gods and goddesses from that pantheon. Thursday, for example, is named for Thor, the Norse god of thunder, strength, and protection (see page 43), while Friday is linked to Freya, goddess of love, fertility, battle, and death. They are always with us, and you can call them down by practicing the ritual described on page 44. You can also add them to shrines and altars in your home. They are sources of strength, and you should feel free to reach out to them in the realm of the unseen. They are there waiting to help you in your life.

Mother Holda

Mother Holda is a maternal, cave-dwelling crone who had power over the weather. One of the more charming tales of her from ancient times is that falling snow came from Mother Holda shaking out her fluffy feather mattress. This wise woman had the additional duty, aside from her climatic work, of nurturing children in her snug cavern home before they were born. Mother Holda represents the very important connection between the generations—crones and babies—which is essential to a healthy culture. Perhaps it is this global grandmother figure that instilled the singularly Scandinavian parenting practice of making sure babies get a few minutes of fresh air every day, if possible, so their lungs become even stronger.

Work with Mother Holda You can tap into Holda's grandmotherly wisdom by stepping outside for a few minutes, no matter what the weather, and breathing the fresh air in deeply. Use at least 10 deep inhales and exhales to signify each decade of a long and healthy life.

Valkyries: Maidens Fierce and Strong

The Valkyries, the nine daughters of Odin in Norse mythology, made many appearances in the Eddas (see page 34). In Old Norse, Valkyries were called "choosers of the dead." The great Viking court entertainers, or *skalds* (see page 34), referred to them as "battle maidens," and they were like angels of death. They who flew over battlefields and chose who was to die. Later, they took on the form of black ravens and flew back to the field of the dead, where they determined who deserved to rise to the status of hero. In old Saxon, they were called "man-eating women" and sometimes appeared as corpse-eating carrion crows. The dead Viking warrior's blood was described by *skalds* as "the raven's drink." The Valkyries then carried the fallen heroes to Valhalla, the great hall of the gods. Those not selected as heroes were left to Freya, goddess of love, fertility, battle, and death, who visited the battlefield in her chariot drawn by cats and took them to her great hall.

The Vikings believed the Valkyries to be beautiful young women who were also fierce and warrior-like, dressed in full battle armor. Valkyries were also capable of shape-shifting: they could disguise themselves as mares or swans and explore the Earth on birds' wings. In the Swedish language, a mare-woman was called a *völva*, a term related to very old Nordic words for the priestesses who conducted ceremonies for the dead, *vila*, *vala*, and *wili* among them (see page 53). Once in Odin's halls, however, they garbed themselves in lovely white robes and gowns. They treated the dead heroes with the respect that was their due: a horn brimming with honeyed mead and a feast. The heroes then became members of Odin's army and spent their next incarnations in even more exciting adventures. One ancient saga in the Poetic Edda, the Grímnismàl, said that the Valkyries' number was thirteen, the number of moons in a year and the number of a coven. The greatest heroes, such as Siegfried, were taken as lovers by Valkyries. Today, witches can invoke a Valkyrie in the gentler form of a swan maiden. Swan maidens were also known as "wish maidens," and you can obtain your truest wish with obeisance to a swan maiden.

WISHING HOUR: NEW MOON VALKYRIE CONJURATION

On any new moon, you can set forth your truest desire with a prayer to the Valkyries, who are the bringers of wishes.

At midnight, which is known as the Witching Hour, go to a table near a window where you can see the moonless night and set out the candle, feather, stone, and fireproof dish. Place the incense in the dish. Light the black candle and the incense, then use the feather to move the smoke as you chant the following:

Valkyrie most fair and bright,

Maiden of power and might,

Bringer of wishes and light,

I call upon you this night

To bring my heart's desire!

At this point, say your wish aloud. Then continue:

So mote it be!

Blessed be thee with gratitude.

Keep waving the incense smoke with the feather and repeat the spell three times. Now extinguish the candle and move this, along with the feather, stone, and dish containing the incense, to your altar for three days. Your wish should begin to manifest at the end of the three days. Remember to thank the wish maiden.

Gather Together

Black candle

Black bird's feather

Black stone such as obsidian or tourmaline

Round fireproof dish to represent the new moon

Frankincense incense

Matches

Sunna

As the ancient Germanic goddess of the sun, Sunna makes it clear that the big star in the sky has not always been deified as male. The Teutons also referred to this very important divine entity as the "Glory of Elves." In Völuspá, a poem found in the great Poetic Edda (see page 34), it was said that she bore a new daughter Suhn, who shed light on a brand-new world. Other sun goddesses include the Arabic Atthar, the Celtic Sulis, and the Japanese Amaterasu.

Work with Sunna As you rise each morning, speak your greeting to Sunna. Morning rituals set a positive tone for the day, ensuring that you are indeed living a magical life.

Odin

Odin is a god of war and death, but also the god of poetry and wisdom. He hung for nine days, pierced by his own spear, on the Yggdrasil, the World Tree. There he learned nine powerful songs and 18 runes. Odin can ask questions of the wisest of the dead and have those questions answered. Equivalent to the Persian Mithra, he is the lord of the underworld and master of wisdom, language, and poetry.

Work with Odin You may successfully appeal to Odin by carving your invocations in runes on candles or through the medium of spoken poetry. Odin can help you with any kind of writing, giving you the energy to forge ahead with purpose and passion. He can even help you write your own rituals and poetic magical chants.

The Norns

The Norns of Scandinavia are some of the older representations of the Triple Goddess, similar to the Moirae of Greek mythology and Saxony's weird sisters. Each Norn was charged with an aspect of fate: past, present, or future, and their motto was, "Become, Becoming, and Shall Be."

They resided in a cave beneath Yggdrasil, the World Tree (see page 60). Dictating the fate of every living thing on Earth, their rule was ultimate, even over the great god Odin. Another part of their domain was the well of Urd. Urd, which is related to the Saxon word *wyrd* or weird, is also the name of the first of the Norns, a manifestation of Mother Earth. Verthandi is the second and Skuld is the last of the Norns, the goddess of death.

Taliesin

This god lives in Wales, the land of "summer stars," and is invoked in higher levels of initiation in some esoteric orders. Taliesin, which means "Shining Brow," is the poet god and harpist; he comes from the Welsh tradition, which is steeped in magic and mystery. He is the wizard's god and embodies wisdom and clairvoyance. Taliesin is an ally to musicians and creative folk.

Work with Taliesen If you are a solo practitioner and want to create a ceremony of self-initiation, Taliesin is a potent power with which to engage.

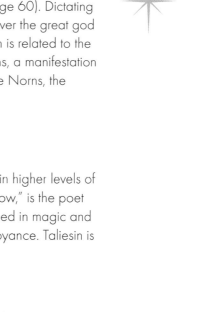

THE FLAME OF LIFE: RITE OF NEEDFIRE

Gather Together

Bowl containing a set of tarot cards

Outdoor altar or table altar

Wood, kindling, matches, and a safe location for a fire

Fire tool or poker

Large candle

Cauldron or large pot

Hot apple cider or warm apple cakes

Vanilla ice cream

Spoons and bowls

Drum for each participant

Without fire, there would be no life. During the Ice Ages, people had to come together in communities to survive, and elements of this ritual recall that time in history, the development of a sacred interdependence, and becoming stronger together. At the core, this rite celebrates life!

Place the bowl of tarot cards on the space designated as the altar. Ask for a volunteer to oversee the fire and act as the leader of the ritual. The fire maker should then select three people to represent the Norns or the Three Fates. One of the fates will be in charge of "giving fire." She lights a candle in the cauldron or pot, then gives it to the fire maker to use to start the main fire. The second fate reads out the future to the ritual participants with a one-card tarot reading. The last fate gives life in the form of the ritual foods—the apples, hot apple cider, and ice cream—served to the participants.

The ritual leader should start the fire and chant the song spell below while the fire is being made. The leader passes a drum to each participant and begins leading rhythmic drumming sounds to underscore the chanting:

Winter winds howl and wail:
we feel the cold in our bones.

This is an old familiar tale.

The ice binds and surrounds us all.

Fates above, please hear our call.

Fire thaws the ice; fire creates the water.

The heat warms our bones.

Fire and ice bind our lives.

Now feel the fire!

Holding hands, everyone then dances slowly around the fire sunwise (that is, clockwise), feeling the life-giving warmth. Next, repeat the chant. The fate of the future goes around the circle with the bowl of tarot cards and performs one card readings for each individual. If time allows, she should also do a reading with the full set of tarot cards for the group about the future of the community.

Lastly, the fate who gives life serves the group celebratory food—the ice cream is a remembrance of the cold of the icy times, while the hot cider or apple cakes represent the life-giving heat of fire. The head of the ritual should then lead everyone in a discussion of the importance of the ritual of the needfire and any other topic important to every participant and the community.

Loki

Thanks to the wildly popular Avengers movie series with superheroes, gods, and goddesses, Loki is well known as a trouble-making trickster god. But he is all of that and more. He is a storyteller and can weave magic spells with his words. He is brilliant and nearly always one step ahead of everyone else. Loki was adopted by Odin but is the son of a frost giant. Loki is truly mischievous and is a creator of chaos.

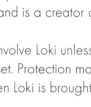

Work with Loki Never involve Loki unless you really want sudden change and upset. Protection magic should be always at the ready when Loki is brought up.

Tyr

The northern European god Tyr lends his name to the third day of the week, Tuesday, or "Tyr's Day." Variations of his name include Tiw in Saxony and Ziu in Germany. Tyr is related to Odin and is known as the god who, more than any other, presides over matters of fairness and law. Tyr is the original Germanic god of war and the patron deity of justice; he was the precursor of Odin. At the time of the Vikings, Tyr had to make way for Odin, who himself became the god of war. Tyr was by then regarded as the son of Odin (or possibly of the giant Hymir). Tyr is represented as a man with one hand since his right hand was bitten off by the gigantic wolf Fenrir (in Old Norse, the wrist was called the "wolf-joint"). His sacred implement is a spear, which is a symbol of justice as well as a weapon.

Work with Tyr Invoke Tyr in rituals that you perform on Tuesdays or for help any time you need to be more aggressive in your job or life. If you are asking for a raise or promotion, or making an entrance at a party, a show of respect to Tyr will abet your bold moves and set you in motion toward success.

Thor

The Norse sky god of thunder, strength, and protection, Thor uses a thunderbolt to enforce his will. Scandinavians of yore believed the crackle of lightning and thunder was Thor's chariot rolling through the heavens. The Norse believed that during a thunderstorm, Thor rode through the heavens on his chariot pulled by two goats, Tanngrisnir (gap-tooth) and Tanngnjóstr (tooth-grinder). Lightning flashed whenever he threw his hammer, Mjöllnir. Thor wears the belt Megingjord, which doubles his already considerable strength. His hall is Bilskirnir, which is in a region called Thrudheim (place of might). His greatest enemy is Jörmungand, the Midgard Serpent or World Serpent. At the day of Ragnarök, or the final destruction of the world, Thor will kill this serpent but die from its poison. His sons will inherit his hammer after his death. Donar is his Teutonic equivalent, while the Romans saw in him their god Jupiter. Thursday is named after him.

Work with Thor Turn to Thor when you need to use spirituality to solve a legal matter. He is also a powerful protection deity to invoke in ritual. Every Thursday, you can—and should—conduct prosperity rituals through prayer and offerings to this ancient northern god of abundance.

CALLING DOWN THE GODS AND GODDESSES: PROTECTION RITUAL

Gather Together

Compass

1 white votive candle

Cedar or pine essential oil

Glass jar

Matches

Frankincense or myrrh incense sticks, whichever feels holiest to you

Piece of paper and a pen

This little spell will take you deep and far inside yourself. It will greatly empower you and instill in you a much deeper understanding of who you are and what you are here to do. Each of us is as individual as a snowflake, and our souls are imprinted with a stamp of specialness. The closer you get to the revelation of your soul's mission, the more you will know why you are here, and more importantly, what you are on Earth to do. That is real magic. The best time to perform this spell is during the darkness of the new moon, when the night sky is at its darkest.

Go outside and find a solitary space in which you can cast a circle. Use the compass to find true north. When you feel comfortable and safe to begin, cast a circle of energy by raising your left hand and, while holding it up high, making a circular motion. Starting at the north point and moving clockwise or sunwise, you will now acknowledge each of the Four Directions (north, east, south, and west) and call in the god and goddess guardians. Stand in the center of the circle, and with your forefinger, anoint your votive candle with the essence of cedar or pine, trees that stay strong, green, and alive all through the winter. Place the candle in the glass jar and light it, setting both carefully and securely on the ground. Then light the incense with the flame of the candle and push it into the ground beside the candle.

Breathe slowly and deeply; make yourself mindful that you are here in the darkest night, celebrating the sacred. As you breathe, look at the majesty of nature and the world around you. Feel the ground beneath your feet. Listen to the silence surrounding you. Now open your heart completely to the awesome power of the universe and the magic both inside and outside of you. Using the same forefinger, anoint your Third Eye, the chakric place above and between your eyes. With your eyes closed, say this rime out loud:

Sitting here beneath the shared sky,

I open my mind and heart and wonder why

I am here; what is my purpose? What shall I try?

Under this moon, tonight, I will learn

The reason why I yearn

To serve the Goddess and the God.

Holy Guardians, I call on you now!

And so it is!

Remain in the center of the circle and keep your eyes closed. You may hear an inner voice, or an outer voice right beside your ear. Listen calmly, staying centered with your two feet on the ground. You will know when it is time to close the circle and leave with your new message and mission. Thank the guardians to seal the sacred space, being sure to leave everything exactly as you found it. Incense, jar, candles, and matches must all leave with you. When you return home, write the message you received on a piece of paper and place this on your altar, where it will be hidden from any eyes but yours. Place the candle, jar, and any remaining incense on your altar. Watch for messages from the guardians as they will surely come within 24 hours.

SOLAR ECLIPSE RITUAL

In Norse mythology, the sun and moon were created by benevolent gods to bring light to a dark world. The Norse gods placed the sun and moon in chariots that flew across the sky, shedding light over the Earth. However, the hungry Fenrir Wolf chased the sun and, every once in a while, caught up with it and devoured it, which darkened the sky. When the sun began to burn the insides of the wolf, he would cough it back into the sky. This, according to Nordic folklore, is how eclipses occur.

Eclipses are celestial events that still fascinate us, and you can easily gather a group together for a ritual when one takes place. Invite enough people to form two circles. Twenty is an ideal number, so you have ten people in each circle. Ask half the people to wear all gold and the other half to wear all black. Those in black are the Fenrir Wolves who will eat the sun, represented by those in gold. For safety, everyone needs to wear their best UV protection sunglasses (in gray, brown, or green) to safeguard their eyes.

Well in advance of the eclipse, form the circles and tell the story of the Fenrir Wolf. Ask other people if they have any experiences of past eclipses that they can share. Ten minutes before the eclipse begins, have the gold group form a circle around the black group. Direct the two circles to walk, dance, or move in opposite directions. Five minutes before the eclipse begins, have the black group move outside the gold circle and have the gold circle sit down.

When I was at a retreat in Mendocino, California, I witnessed people barking, howling, and moaning to express their roles and the immense power of this imminent heavenly happening. During the actual eclipse, however, everyone tends to grow silent and experience the extraordinary power of this rare and sacred heavenly moment. As always, people should only look at the sun through special filters. The best way to experience this ritual is to sit with eyes closed and feel its immensity.

In about ten minutes, as the eclipse is occurring, the black-garbed folks should walk away, at least 10 feet (3 m), one by one, and sit in a circle. When the gold circle is the only group left, this symbolizes the full reappearance of the sun.

When people begin to stir and want to talk, ask everyone to share what came to mind. People often have amazing insights and visions during eclipses. Document these "eclipse epiphanies," if possible, and remember to include them in your storytelling for the next solar eclipse ritual.

Fairy Enchantment: Magic on Gossamer Wings

Fairies have long been described in the legends and lore of nearly every culture. The fairy world is naturally the province of Norse magic. While the appearance of fairies varies greatly from culture to culture, these gossamer beings are generally genial, gentle, and magical in and of themselves. Fairies can appear as golden-haired maidens, hideous hags, black maws of bad and malevolent energy, a fleeting shadow, a golden glinting in the distance, or even as natural phenomena such as twinkling lights in the sky, a rustling sound, conspicuous and surprising in the leaves, or a rippling of the water when there is no wind. They seem to be members of the same family, scattered over the Earth and throughout history, but somehow all in league with each other. Whether harpy hags or beautiful blondes wafting through the woods, Lord of the Rings-style fairies have long been believed in, sight unseen—they are invisible entities, unseen yet altogether powerful. For centuries, country folk placated the fairy world with offerings of cookies, flowers, and a special cup of sparkling cider.

Puddlefoot: Brownie of the Burn

It is my personal theory that no less an author than J. R. R. Tolkien himself was inspired by this spirit to create the character Gollum. Puddlefoot is a nature spirit who comes from one place only: a farm in Scotland. He was like a helper spirit; when not splashing around in his favorite pond, or burn, as they are called locally, he did housecleaning on the farm. Unfortunately, Puddlefoot never wiped his feet and usually made more of a mess. Once, a drunken Scot greeted him by name and thus caused Puddlefoot to disappear forever. Akin to the legends of Rumpelstiltskin and Tom Tit Tot, to name a spirit is to employ the power to send it away.

Meremaidens: Water Deities

These water spirits are perhaps the most legendary of all the fairy folk, for an obvious reason: mermaids usually appear as spectacularly beautiful women. From the waist up, they are lovely and lithe females, and from the waist down they are fish. Meremaidens, usually known as mermaids, have been a part of the fabric of our myth and folklore for centuries. The most common image conjured is that of a lovely lady sitting on a rock by the side of a sea or lake, often with her fish tail hidden by the water. The word meremaid means "maiden of the sea." They make themselves known by their sultry singing, which can act as a lure to any men passing within earshot of their songs; this links them with sirens. Sirens, however, seduce seafarers with their singing and usually lead them to their doom. From Homer to the fairy tales of Hans Christian Andersen, mermaids are supernatural beings who perform important roles, from warning of disaster to bestowing unforgettable gifts. Having said that, rescuing a mermaid comes at your own risk.

Nidhogg: The Dragon of Envy

Beware this malicious being of Scandinavian lore; he is a lord of the underworld who threatens the very existence of the world by chewing on the deep underground roots of the Tree of Life—Yggdrasil, also called the World Tree (see page 60)—and the bodies of the dead. Nidhogg translates as "Envy Dragon," which hints at the dark heart of this nether-dwelling creature. In our lives, envy can be a natural human emotion, but it is not healthy and can leave you feeling unhappy. When Nidhogg first begins to show his dragon head, immediately do some letting go and reframe your sense of jealousy into something else, such as awareness, appreciation, a spirit of generosity, that will raise your vibration instead of lowering it. Send the Envy Dragon flying away!

Fairy Invitation Invocation

It is very wise to be careful about asking the fairies to enter your life as they can also cause a little mischief, but a very conscious invitation can invite only the best aspects of fairy energy into your life. Go outside your home, ideally into the backyard or onto a deck or stoop (outside steps), and say the following out loud:

Friends of the Fairy Realm,

I call upon you

To bring your magic

Into my life.

I welcome your good energy

And protection to my home.

Fairy Friends, bring bright blessings!

Now clap three times and repeat the last line of the spell. Keep your eyes peeled as blessing will arrive soon!

RINGS OF PEACE SPELL
FOR RESTLESS SPIRITS

Gather Together

Box of ground cinnamon

Cinnamon incense

Matches

On visiting somewhere new, many of us have experienced the feeling that the energy is just off—a feeling of sadness pervades the space perhaps. It could well be that a sour or unhappy spirit has settled in and is making its presence known. You can help this restless entity let go and move on in peace with this simple spell. It is good to feel pity and compassion for restless and unhappy spirits. So, instead of ignoring the unfortunate and unseen entity, perform this spell to put them at ease and enable them to make their way somewhere else and find peace at long last.

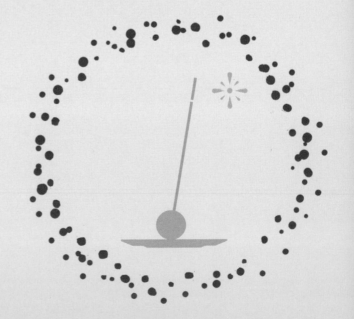

Go outside your home or to a nearby park or woods. Take the box of cinnamon and create a ring of at least a few feet in diameter. Stand in the center of the ring and say the following spell out loud:

Dear Unseen Friend,

You long for peace of mind,

You long for peace at heart.

I wish for you a respite from your trouble,

I wish for you nothing but joy in your journey.

Step into this ring and accept the blessings,

Step out of this ring filled with blessings for your journey.

You are released from all unrest,

You are released from your troubles.

Blessings for your journey. Blessed be thee!

Now step out of the circle, light the incense, and place it in the center of the ring. Say the spell again as the incense burns down. Once the incense has burned down, the newly peace-filled spirit will leave for greener and happier pastures. Make sure the incense is extinguished safely and leave the circle of protection, which will soon return to the earth and leave security and blessings behind.

HONORING THE DEITY WITHIN: NEW MOON SMOKE BLESSING

Gather Together

Bonfire or firepot

Pipe with very mild tobacco

"Gifts of wisdom" for the new moon mage

Nontoxic face paint or makeup

Feathers, leather, and beads for a new headdress

Drums

This ritual is best performed on the night of a new moon. It is to honor a new member and welcome them to your group.

Gather together the tribe or your spiritual group or coven and form a seated circle around the fire. Honor the new member, or mage (a person with magical knowledge), with stories. You are encouraged to tell any tales of courage, honesty, and generosity, as these reveal the best qualities of the group to your new friend. After story time, pass the pipe around for the blessing of smoke. Present the new tribal member with a name and provide an explanation of this. For example, "I name you 'Lady Moonwater' because you are wise and reflective, because you shine." The new name should have a mythic aspect, and be one of great respect, deifying the person with something truly honorific. (For further name inspiration, see pages 56–57.)

The tribe should welcome the newly christened person by going around the circle and speaking their blessings and hopes for their future, such as: "Lady Moonwater, may you see the world and find the place that speaks most deeply to your heart."

Now is the time to present the newly named tribal member with the gifts of wisdom. We are not speaking here of expensive new toys or watches, but a book that changed your life and the reason why, or an amber amulet for protection. Next, the tribe should decorate the celebrant with face paint or makeup and make a headdress with feathers, leather, and beads. They should make the headdress together and ensure it is as magnificent as possible. This headdress is the insignia of newfound status within the tribe.

Drum and sing on this new moon night, as an important new member of the tribe has just come into being!

Our Sacred Shamanic Lineage: Wild Seidr Women

In Norse mythology, the goddess Freya was a practitioner of *seidr*, which is defined as a form of pre-Christian Norse magic and shamanism (a practice that is regarded as having access to, and influence in, the world of good and evil spirits). Seidr attempts to direct the course of fate, working from within to bring about change by symbolically weaving new events into existence. Freya was also a *völva*, which is a professional or semi-professional practitioner of seidr. It was Freya who first brought this art to the Norse gods. As a *völva*, Freya wandered from place to place, performing acts of magic in exchange for various types of compensation. As a shaman in her own right, a *völva* was both revered and ridiculed in society. This is the experience of many women in their daily lives: we are constantly placed in a box and judged for our choices. Like the *völva*, we give but we often don't receive the appreciation we deserve.

However, the *völva* is also reminiscent of the *veleda*, a seeress or prophetess who held a more clearly defined and highly respected position among Germanic tribes. In either of these roles, the female practitioner of these arts was seen as a dignified individual. So, in some instances, these stories do cast women in a positive light.

As women we encounter endless challenges throughout our lives. But I believe experiencing struggle in the world every day has instilled us with an inner strength that is unmatched by our male counterparts. We have a sense of being that provides the navigation necessary for life. Women can use this spiritual energy and harness it to determine the journey that lies ahead. Female shamans throughout history have used various materials to connect to the spirit world. A very wise friend of mine hosts a group of drummers, using instruments repurposed from leather and sheepskin and decorated with objects found in nature. Using these drums, they channel powerful cleaning and healing energy.

Such instincts are inside each of us—we just need to use the methods and objects left by others to connect with and bring forth lost energy. Our thoughts, words, and actions can all determine our fate as well as that of others. We must look inside ourselves and pay close attention to where the spiritual world wants to take us. We have the power to choose our path and it is our destiny to allow the spirit world to guide us.

SHAMANIC SMOKE SPELL: CONJURING YOUR SPIRIT GUIDES

Gather Together

Amber incense

Matches

Fireproof dish or holder for the incense

Large tray to hold all the items

Black votive candle

Amber essential oil

Palo Santo incense

Sage bundle for smudging

Small metal cauldron or large fireproof dish

I have been told that one of the surest ways to connect with other energies is to burn incense. One of my mentors, the European witch Zsuzsanna Budapest, told me: "The spirits like smoke; it can slip between our worlds. Burn it as an offering and anytime you want to connect to the other side." I have lived by her words and know you will benefit from her wisdom in your own magical workings.

On a Friday, the day that is sacred to the goddess Freya, light some amber incense and place it on the tray. Anoint yourself and the candle with amber essential oil and then light the candle. Take a deep breath and inhale the sacred scent, which is born of nature and gifts to us from the trees. Now light the Palo Santo incense and sage with the candle and place these in the cauldron or dish. Put the cauldron or dish and the candle on the tray. As you watch the smoke billow from the cauldron and candle, say the following spell out loud:

In this hallowed day,

Sacred to the Goddess,

I call upon the ancestors

For guidance and guidance.

Help me to see the way forward

As I walk the path on this earthly plane.

Help me to gather wisdom on my way.

Bring me visions and the gift of sign.

Deep gratitude to you, beloved ancestors.

You are welcome here and now.

And so it is; blessed be.

Carry the tray, which is a mobile altar, all around your home, so the entire space is imbued with the energy of the sanctified smoke and to welcome benevolent spirits into your home. To close the spell, place the tray on your main altar and repeat the spell. Extinguish the flames and stay alert for messages from beyond. Whenever you feel the need for council from elders from the other side, repeat the ritual.

The Rite of Naming: Embracing Our Mythology

You can create a wild and wonderful name for yourself using the unique Mythic Name Generator shown in the tables (there's one for men and one for women). To use a table, you can either close your eyes and point or use two six-sided dice. Roll the dice to pick a title from column A, a name from column B, an occupation from column C, and subjects from column D. With any luck, you just might end up with a fantastic name like "Empress Nocturna, Keeper of the Ravens" or "Master Byron, Liberator of Clergymen."

Mythic Name Generator—Male

	(A) TITLE	(B) NAME	(C) OCCUPATION	(D) SUBJECTS
1	Most	Awesome	Brewer	Trolls
2	Prince	Crow	Creator	Ravens
3	Lord	Dracul	Releaser	Seraphim
4	Count	Spider	Moonwatcher	Innocents
5	Baron	Bold One	Destroyer	Bats
6	Father	Sebastian	Nightbringer	Angels
7	Priest	Onyx	Liberator	Maidens
8	Sir	Byron	Soulmender	Clergymen
9	Master	Diablo	Avenger	Dead
10	Duke	Darkness	Sentry	Crypt
11	Emperor	Barnabas	Necromancer	Succubae
12	Darth	Nocturnus	Night Guardian	Spiders

Mythic Name Generator—Female

	(A) TITLE	(B) NAME	(C) OCCUPATION	(D) SUBJECTS
1	Highness	Amber	Healer	Fairies
2	Princess	Acacia	Seductress	Night
3	Lady	Selkie	Keeper	Owls
4	Madame	Lilith	Enchantress	Seraphim
5	Mother	Golden	Priestess	Innocents
6	Countess	Amethyst	Usurper	Ravens
7	Mistress	Malora	Magical One	Angels
8	Dame	Lucina	Eradicator	Devils
9	Czarina	Magdalena	Wielder of Power	Nobles
10	Marquesa	Isis	Bringer of Justice	Black Veil
11	Queen	Freya	Watcher	All
12	Empress	Nocturna	Webmistress	Spiders

Chapter 3

FOREST FOLKLORE

The World Tree, Yggdrasil, was the foundation of the universe in Norse lore. Harness the power of trees for protection, love, abundance, wellbeing, and more.

The World Tree: The Roots of Sylvan Magic

The mythos of the Norse is rooted in one tree, Yggdrasil, or the World Tree. Even movies, namely *Thor*, part of the Marvel series, have referenced this core aspect of Norse lore and legend: all the world and every realm comes from this single tree. This massive ash tree is at the center of the universe. Its great branches rise above the heavens and the trunk is deeply secured in the ground by three giant roots. It is here that the pantheon of gods, goddesses, and other magical beings gather and manage the nine realms of existence, even that of earthbound mortals. It is said that all sustenance comes from Yggdrasil. Indeed, the early Norse needed trees to survive: to provide food, shelter, fire, and so much more, including inspiration and refuge. That has remained a constant through the millennia for humans—trees are essential for life. In the past few decades, we have come to realize just how crucial trees are to life on Earth. They are the "lungs of the planet," enabling us to breathe and survive, and protecting them has become more important and urgent than ever before. Trees are holy beings, to be treasured, honored, and planted, and for making sacred magic.

FOREST FLOOR EARTHING

The grounding ritual of earthing has grown in popularity. Taking off your shoes and feeling the energy of Mother Earth beneath your feet will center you like nothing else. The earth in a forest is blessed with the additional enchantment of trees and so you should ground yourself in this whenever you find yourself in the woods. Doing this at the weekend will bring you so much serenity.

On a Sunday, walk to a nearby forest or wood. If it is far enough that you need to drive or take a ride there, once you are close enough, make sure to at least take a brief walk to the forest. Once you are there, go deep enough into the forest to ensure you're surrounded by trees on all sides. Take off your shoes and socks and feel the dirt, leaves, tree needles, and richness of the ground on the soles of your feet.

Speak this enchantment aloud:

Mother of us All,
I stand upon you
Gaining strength,
Gaining hope.
I stand upon you
As the life flows through me.
I honor the web of life
That connects us all:
Tree, flower, leaf, and seeds.
To you, we owe all things.
Blessed be thee.
Thank you, Mother Earth.
To you, we owe all life.

Pick up a pretty fallen leaf, pine cone, or acorn from the forest floor. As you go about your day after this rite and respite, carry the inner peace and sense of the sacred with you. Place the memento of forest floor earthing on your altar and remember the tranquility you felt.

Your Magical Grove: A Guide to Sacred Trees

It is no coincidence that the beginning of your journey with tree magic is very similar to the start of a walk through a forest. At first, only a few common trees are recognizable, and it's easy to seek those out among the unfamiliar ones. But the deeper you wander, the more usual it is to suddenly look up and find there are new trees around you that you would never have noticed if you had stayed at the edge of the forest. Like any great adventure, the best discoveries are made by those brave enough to embrace what they did not know before.

The history of tree magic dates back far beyond what we can know from recorded annals as early peoples undoubtedly performed rituals with trees. Consider ancient Celtic beliefs. The Celts were an early Indo-European people who spread across Europe during the 1st century BCE. However, history remembers the Celts most clearly as a result of the places where their language and culture has remained strongest—namely, in Ireland and Scotland. According to Celtic belief, people were drawn to forests for more than practical reasons, such as taking shelter or collecting the abundant wood for kindling and building fires. They also believed that the trees created the people and were thus what kept them alive.

Over the course of time, a belief in the magical properties of trees began to grow and evolve, as did the number of people who held this view. Thus appeared the Druids, a term used to describe this new group of believers which is derived from a Latin transcription of an ancient Celtic word meaning "knower of the oak tree." The Druids believed that the Tree of Life was not the only tree to possess sacred gifts, but that all trees have mystical properties.

The Druids turned to the forest and found that, hidden within the roots of the tallest elder tree and from within the branches of the tiniest sapling, was magic. Mystical legends were attached to the origins of each type of tree, as were a list of the trees' qualities that could help a person in need of assistance. For example, a birch tree could ward off evil and protect against attacks, while a willow tree became a symbol of rebirth and regeneration for emotional balance in life. Those who practice Druidry (or Druidism) turn to nature in times of personal conflict, whether great or small, and take great care to protect forests from destruction. Even today, if you go hiking, you might meet a Druid meditating in the forest and communicating with the trees through the language of Ogham. Ogham is itself an ancient language that stems back to the 6th century CE and consists of simple strokes that help a person communicate with the natural world. The Druids believe a soul can find harmony from within by communicating with the Earth. In fact, it is only when I feel my bare feet on the solid earth or have my eyes properly drinking in a space flourishing with leaves and greenery, that I truly feel as though my restless desire has been fulfilled.

Let's take these first steps into the forest together. Take your time, breathe in deeply, and you'll find you're ready to begin. Here are a few ideas for how you can use trees to enhance your own wellbeing.

For healing

Pine tree
- Carry the cones to increase fertility
- Burn the needles to reverse spells
- Scatter on the floor to reject evil
- Place a branch over the bed to cure sickness
- Use pine essential oil to speed up healing, attract money, increase magical energy, and cure negative thoughts

Magnolia tree
- Helps your immune system and fights off illness or sorrow
- Bestows blessings of feminine strength
- Known as the Mother Goddess tree
- Preaches self-confidence and the ability to stay true to yourself

Palo Santo tree
- Burn to cleanse and add positive energy to a space
- Use as a sacred, holy wood
- Relieves stress and anxiety
- Eliminates headaches and cold
- Enhances creativity
- Calms the immune system

Sandalwood tree
- Provides spirituality, healing, and protection
- Releases a powerful vibration that helps with spirituality
- Keeps you enlightened and grounded
- Use as a base in incense for healing during full moons

Linden (lime) tree
- Wands made from linden have healing properties
- Connected to light and positivity
- Good for medicines and healing
- Use for the purposes of white magic

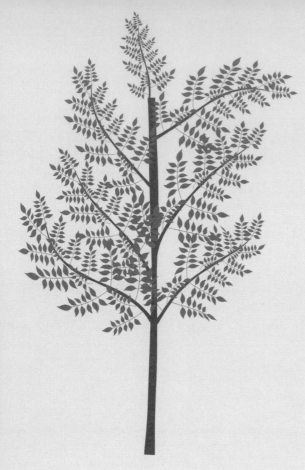

For protection

Rowan tree

- Regarded as a symbol of tenacity
- Carries berries with a tiny, five-pointed star resembling a pentagram on the bottom, giving the tree magical properties
- Wards off evil forces
- Offers protection when worn, hung in doorways, or planted

Spruce tree

- Known as the protector
- Aids those on the path of healing, or hoping to create a sacred/safe space
- Provides spiritual/energetic protection for those dealing with negative energy

Juniper tree

- Guards against bad magic
- Provides relief from physical pain
- Known for providing good luck and protection
- Used in rituals for blessings or purification
- Helps with manifestations

Holly tree

- Symbolizes eternal life
- Provides protection against thunder, lightning, and demons when planted near the house
- Has formidable associations with protection and warfare

For wisdom / knowledge

Ash tree

- Regarded as the Tree of Life
- Believed to cure warts
- Holds understanding, empathy, and universal knowledge

Hazel tree

- Has wisdom
- Helps divine underground water
- Hazelnuts from this tree make for a powerful dowsing pendulum

Laurel tree

- Helps with achievements, creativity, and inspiration
- Protects against illness
- Symbolizes peace and growth

Birch tree
- Protective in warding off evil
- Builds courage
- Good for wand making
- Protects against psychic attack
- Helps maintain balance and compassion
- Allows deep connection with the Earth, which helps promote gentleness

Cedar tree
- Use to cleanse negative atmospheres
- Creates sacred spaces
- Aids the summoning of helpful spirits for rituals and invocations

For love

Sycamore tree
- Enhances development, perseverance, and vitality
- Promotes relaxation and harmony, while at the same time raising energy levels and banishing lethargy
- Good for magic linked to love, prosperity, and longevity

Apple tree
- Associated with hedge witches
- Regarded as the Tree of Love and Knowledge
- Good for beginner witches making a wand

Rosewood tree
- Said to bring true and everlasting love
- Useful for love divination
- Provides protection of a loved one
- Ideal for love spells and blessings

Cherry tree
- Makes a great wand for love magic
- Good for divination spells
- Can bring calm to heated situations
- Creates passion

PASSION FRUIT: LOVE SPELL
WITH CHERRY FRUIT

Gather Together

*Square of pink cloth,
9 x 9 inches (23 x 23 cm)*

Pen with red ink

9 cherries

2 rose quartz stones

Small red dish

Use cherry tree magic to bring lasting love into your life.

Fill your mind with thoughts of love and visualize your prospective partner. On one side of the piece of cloth, in the center, draw two large overlapping hearts in red ink. Pick up two cherries. Place them in the center of the hearts and say, "This represents true and mutual love." Pick up two more cherries and say, "This represents a loving and equal exchange." Pick up two more and say, "These two for truth and loyalty." Pick up two more and say, "These stand for the bloom of good health and endurance." Pick up the last cherry and say, "This sweet fruit stands for the everlasting bond that unites us. May it stay strong for all eternity." Take the rose quartz stones, place them with the cherries, and say, "May this love stand the test of time and be set for all eternity... and so it is."

Now eat the cherries and put the pits (stones), which are the cherry seeds, in the red dish, then place this in your bedroom along with the two rose quartz stones and the cloth for at least nine days. All the while, the seeds will be emanating the energy of the true love coming your way.

Tree Essences

On reflection, I realize that one of the greatest blessings of my life was growing up on a farm. I remember complaining as a teenager about living "out in the sticks" but, thankfully, that was a brief phase. Daily walks in the woods kept me grounded and growing herbs and wild crafting in fields and meadows gave me a sense of purpose. These activities also taught me the importance of being self-sufficient. Once I had learned how to work with herbs, flowers, and essential oils and extracts, I realized that our Mother Earth is constantly generating healing energy for us to apply to our lives. I also learned the very important lesson that we are here to help others. Essential oils are true helpmates that we can use daily for health, work, prosperity, success, mental clarity, and happier homekeeping. Below are some suggestions for how to use various essential oils to enhance your life.

Fir oil

Also known as Balm of Gilead, fir oil comes from the balsam fir tree (*Abies balsamea*). It has been in use since ancient times and is associated with forest spirits and tree magic. The Druids claimed that it helped with shape-shifting. It is an awakening essential oil and rebalances the heart and mind.

Spruce oil

Known also as black spruce (*Picea mariana*), this rich and woodsy oil can promote mental clarity in the user. It is also very grounding for when you are feeling scattered. This oil was used as a medicinal by Native Americans who valued the positive effects it had on mind, body, and spirit. Inhaling the scent from a mist-spray bottle or diffuser can aid breathing, relax you, and help you sleep. You can use the oil in purification rituals, as did the Native Americans.

Western red cedar oil

This has a strong, woody, and refreshing aroma and is a powerful essential oil to use for grounding. The oil can also be used in nature spells and when working with forest and plant deities and energies. It promotes longevity and can help retain youthful looks and energy. If you want to connect with Mother Earth, use Western red cedar oil.

Juniper berry oil

This essential oil has a feminine energy and is sacred to earth deities. It has a sweet and woody aroma that makes it great in aromatherapy and as an anointing application. It can also be used for its strong clearing properties before spellwork.

Amber oil

Derived from the resin of tree sap, the delightful scent of this essential oil indicates that it contains much magic and is excellent for love spells. Amber oil will ground and balance your personal energy. Amber is also beneficial for purification, psychic shielding, and protection.

Frankincense oil

This is an ancient essence that was long considered precious. An earthy and woody oil, it is perfect for clearing blocked nasal passageways to promote better breathing. Native to regions of Northern Africa, you can enjoy the oil's benefits by inhaling it or massaging it into pressure points. It is prized for use in magical workings and highest rituals, such as sabbats and seasonal holy days. It also keeps evil away.

Tea tree oil

This has been used by the Aborigines in Australia for centuries and has powerful antibacterial, antifungal, and antiseptic properties. It has a fresh camphor smell and is used for space clearing and energy management. It can swiftly rid your home of negative energy and be used to ward off malevolent spirits. Use tea tree essential oil to clear out and reset vibrations after an illness.

Scandinavian Tree Potion Self-Care: DIY Nature Cures

Here are two simple beauty recipes for you to try. Keep some sealable glass jars with lids handy, so you can store them for up to two months. Always remember to rinse your shower, bathtub, and sink well after use to avoid stains, rings, or stickiness.

The Sweet Life: Amber Bath Salts

Glass or ceramic bowl
Airtight, sealable jar
½ cup (120 g) Epsom salts
2 tablespoons orange juice and 1 teaspoon orange zest
1 tablespoon almond oil
4 tablespoons amber essential oil

Combine all the ingredients thoroughly in the bowl and store in an airtight, sealable jar. Amber oil is so sensual and will make you feel as if you are enveloped in love. These salts are perfect for a bath before a romantic evening.

Frankincense Bath Sugar

Glass or ceramic bowl
Airtight, sealable jar
1 cup (200g) brown sugar
3 tablespoons melted coconut oil
1 teaspoon each of ground cinnamon and ground cloves
2 tablespoons frankincense essential oil

Mix all the ingredients thoroughly in the bowl and store in an airtight, sealable jar, or use in one weekend since it makes enough for two baths. This holy combination will imbue you with a sense of the sacred.

ROOTED IN SELF: A START-YOUR-DAY SPELL

This spell will ground you in yourself, with calm, clarity, and the wonderful energy of a tree. Every single morning is sacred; you should acknowledge this as often as possible and it's a marvelous way to start each day. This blessing will imbue your day with self-love and a strong sense of the importance of spirituality in your life.

Go to your bathtub or shower and put everything you need on a tray. Light the candle, then anoint it with the vanilla essential oil. Next, light the incense using the candle and say the spell aloud:

Goddess, bless this day,

Goddess, bless me, I pray.

As the sun rises this morning,
I feel the warmth of each ray.

May health, happiness, and love
surround me as I make my way
this day.

So mote it be.

Gather Together

Tray

Yellow candle

Matches

Vanilla essential oil

Vanilla incense stick

1 cup of body scrub or either of the spa scrubs on page 69

Step into your bathtub or shower and test the bath scrub on your inner wrist first to make sure it doesn't irritate your skin. If safe to proceed, slather the scrub gently all over your body and leave it on while you repeat the words from the spell. Rinse off the scrub and visualize yourself going through your day surrounded by blessings on what will surely be a beautiful day. After you have toweled yourself dry and before you get dressed, extinguish the candle and dab the vanilla oil on the pulse points behind your ears, on your neck, on your inner wrists, and behind your knees. As you make your way through the day, you will leave a lovely, blessing-filled scent in your wake.

Supernatural Sylvan Secrets

We can turn to the trees of the forest to improve our lives and wellbeing. Follow the suggestions below and see the benefits of using the power of tree magic to enhance your life.

Juniper tree

- Carry a bowl of smoking juniper needles throughout the home to cleanse the areas where spirits may lurk, especially in the corners.
- Place fresh juniper boughs over the front door and windows to protect the home from unwanted entities or spells.
- Use a dab of juniper essential oil on used items you purchase to send away the unwanted vibrations of the former owner.
- Once a month, at the new moon, use a juniper smudging bundle to cleanse your space of anything negative.
- Cleanse crystals in a bowl of juniper needles or add to a steamy bath.

Willow tree

- Use willow branches, leaves, or bark in new moon practices to increase psychic abilities.
- Willow is connected to female fertility and can be used in spellwork to increase creativity, assist through the passages of life, attract love, and bring about deep healing from emotional pain. Honor the moon to increase the quantity of love in your life. Braid three willow branches together on a new moon and bend them to form a circle. Secure the ends with red or pink ribbon and place by your bed to attract a true love. Willows bend to your desires.

Linden (lime) tree

- Use linden flowers for love spells and add them to incense.
- Dried linden flowers mixed with lavender and lemon blossoms placed in a sachet will induce sleep.
- Use dried linden leaves in a smudge stick, or add to a bowl, for purification.
- Fresh linden flowers placed in a room will keep all spirits healthy and vibrant.
- If you dream of a linden tree, your marriage or love relationship is in grave danger.
- Use linden essential oil for making prophecies and connecting with the seer inside you.

MONEY DRAWING POTION: PROSPERITY TREE SPELL

The grounded energy and rooted stability of trees makes them ideal for spellwork regarding abundance. Also, the color green is associated with wealth and most trees have an abundance of green leaves, while some even have green bark and flowers. All this makes trees perfect for conjuring cash!

Place the coins in the bowl and put the crystals on top of them. To make the potion, use the mortar and pestle to grind up the maple leaves until you have about 3 teaspoons of ground leaf. Add 3 teaspoons of sugar to the ground leaves and grind well, ensuring everything is nicely combined. Then sprinkle the herbal potion on top of the coins and crystals in the bowl. Place the bowl on your altar and say aloud:

Abundance finds me and brings bounty to me

On this day and every day.

Prosperity is on the way!

So mote it be.

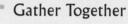

Gather Together

Handful of coins, ideally very shiny new pennies, nickels, and dimes (depending on which country you are in)

Small, green bowl

3 green crystals such as peridot or jade

Mortar and pestle

5 large, dry maple leaves

¼ cup (50 g) granulated sugar

How to Use a Tree Branch Wand for Magic

Your magic wand will probably find you one day as you walk in the woods. Ideally, it will be a fallen branch on the forest floor. Wands are excellent energy conductors that can be used for casting spells, healing, and summoning spirits, and even finding water if you want to have a go at dowsing! Here are a few tips to try when preparing your wand for magical work.

- Cleanse your wand using crystals, earth, fir needles, music, sage, cedar chips, moonlight, sunlight, or water.
- Set your intention for the kind of activity you are about to commence. Say this aloud. For escape, it can be: Purify this space here and now. So mote it be!
- Hold your wand in your right hand for invoking, summoning, praying, or chanting. Hold the wand in your left hand when banishing or dismissing negative spirits. (If you are left-hand dominant, reverse the positions.)
- Spell out your intention in the air using the wand as you would use a pen for writing.
- You can also use the wand for healing. Point the wand at the physical issue or concern without touching the area. Make circular motions over the area while reciting a prayer, mantra, or incantation. Allow the energy to transfer from the wand to the person or animal to shower healing energy over them.
- Never rush a spell. Allow the outcome to occur in time naturally
- Conclude by thanking all the gods and goddesses, fairies, and nature spirits who partook in the magical session.
- Keep your wand(s) in a safe and sacred place. Cover it with a purple cloth and keep it away from public contact. Recharge the wand before your next magical session.

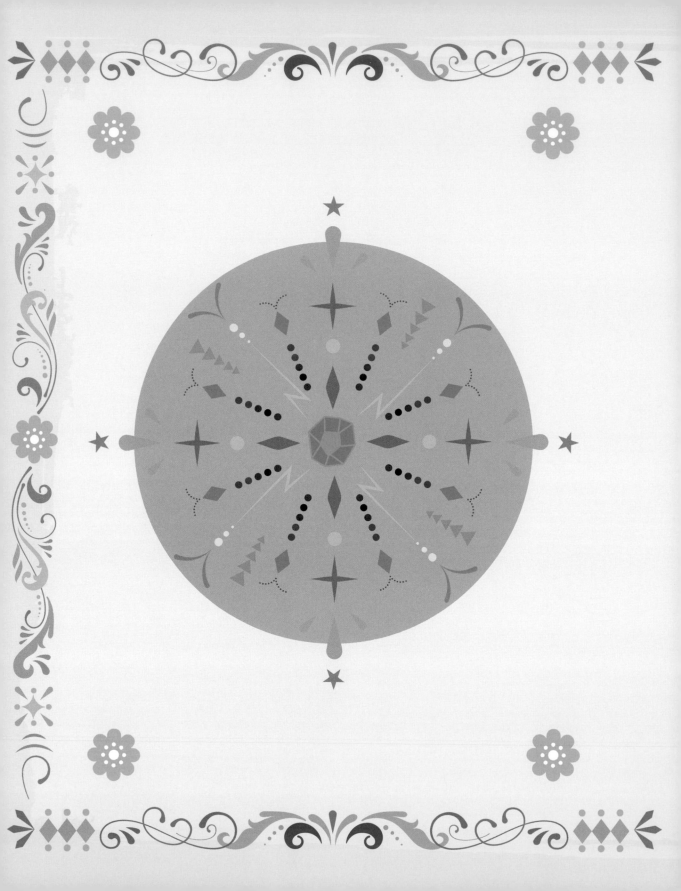

Chapter 4

CRYSTAL ENCHANTMENTS AND HEALING

Precious stones are filled with special energy. Learn about their uses
in magic and ritual, from boosting confidence and offering clarity
to aiding meditation and divination.

The Power of Sacred Stones to Enhance Your Entire Life

During my childhood, I loved walking around woods looking for flowers, rocks, and all manner of trees. Pretty crystals with unusual shapes or colorations would catch my eye, and I would come back home from my Thoreau-esque wanderings with my pockets filled. At the age of 11, I read J. R. R. Tolkien's *The Hobbit* and then immediately dived into *The Lord of the Rings*. Now, Tolkien understood the power of crystals and gems, and he contributed greatly to their legend and lore. I remember reading enviously about the Dwarves' glittering caves and treasure troves. For me, it was no mystery that the One Ring was evil, because it was a plain band inscribed with the language of Mordor in Elvish script and with no stones at all, while the rings of the heroic Elrond, Gandalf, Galadriel, and Aragorn all featured beautiful stones.

So, stones and gems were good and had the power to help vanquish evil? Yep, this I could completely understand. Even in the lavish and incredibly entertaining movie versions of this epic book series, stones have a starring role; I think I especially enjoyed when Gandalf claps a big quartz crystal onto his wizard's staff to light the way. I was also delighted to discover that Tolkien's Middle Earth was akin to Europe and England, covering much of the north. Indeed, the great scribe's fantasy was largely informed by his study of the folklore of what is now Scandinavia, whose people prized metals, fossils, petrified tree crystals, and all manner of magical rocks. The Norse were a practical people with a passion for the sacred. They had to be pragmatic to survive the cold, harsh northern climate for many months, but every aspect of their life was enhanced by Mother Nature's gift of gems and crystals. This mythos and magical intent were woven into their traditions. For example, amber, the crystal formed from a tree's golden resin, is known as "Freya's Tears" and regarded as holy and healing to widows, while diamonds are sparks of Thor's lightning. This reverence for gems and crystals appears throughout Norse magic.

Beryl—The Power Stone

The 13th-century medieval historian Arnoldus Saxo noted that warriors would use beryl to help them in battle and reported that it was good for court cases. However, his declaration that the wearer of a beryl stone was made unconquerable and smarter, and cured of any laziness, perhaps borders on the hyperbole! Bartholomaeus Anglicus' German classic *De Proprietatibus Rerum* (On the Properties of Things) spoke of the power of the beryl stone to reawaken the love of married couples. Early crystal balls were frequently made of polished beryl spheres, rather like the palantirs used by J. R. R. Tolkien's wizards. The Druids and Celts used beryl to divine the future, and legend has it that Merlin, King Arthur's magician, carried a beryl ball around with him for exactly that purpose.

Work with beryl Beryl has the marvelous property of helping you to avoid the unnecessary. Thus, a beryl crystal will make you more efficient and bring you simplicity and greater peace of mind. When stress appears in your life, carry a beryl crystal in your pocket or wear it as a pendant to achieve quietude quickly.

Flint: The Fairies' Favorite

Flint is beloved by the fairy folk. If you want to stay on the good side of the wee ones, and believe me it is advisable to do this, keep at least one piece of flint around. They will be pleased with you for having their favorite stone and will go about their own business and not meddle in yours. If you have lots of little problems like keys going missing and losing your wallet, invest in some flint as soon as possible!

Onyx for Optimism

Onyx possesses a lot of earth energy, as shown by its usually very dark, often black, color. It has been used for centuries, even in building and for weapons (in the form of arrowheads in the northern kingdoms). Onyx holds memories and secrets, retaining a physical record of what happens around it; therefore, it can be regarded as a story stone. It is super stable and shares this strength with people who need it. It is particularly good for athletes and those who do physical labor. Healers recommend that onyx be worn only on the left side of the body, or on a chain so it hangs at the center of the body over the heart or solar plexus areas. Onyx is best for relieving stress and quietening the mind. This is a generous rock in that it creates goodwill and self-confidence.

Work with onyx I give talks at metaphysical bookstores and conferences, which can make me worry whether I will do a good job, explain myself well, and do justice to the topic. I have an onyx bracelet that I wear for these occasions which gives me the confidence I need. If you have a forthcoming event that is making you nervous, or a very thorny or difficult task at hand, adorn yourself with an onyx ring, bracelet, or pendant—things will run more smoothly and you'll feel more optimistic about what you're facing as a result.

LOKI-PROOF YOUR LIFE WITH LODESTONE

Lodestone, the polarized version of magnetite, was believed to provide protection against spells and other magical mischief, such as that created by Loki (see page 42). The ancients also believed that a tiny piece of lodestone beneath the pillow would help the person sleeping on top of it to become more virtuous. Alexander the Great gave his soldiers lodestone to defend them against unseen evil spirits.

Diamonds—Fragments of the Stars

I love the charming legend that Europeans first discovered diamonds from Africa in the pouch of a shaman, who used them for healing magic. Prehistoric peoples believed diamonds were fragments of the stars and the teardrops of the gods. In very ancient times, they were worn as adornment in their rough and unpolished state. As you might imagine, they are thought to bring good luck, but there is another school of thought, held by diamond-phobes, that these gems bring misfortune. The legend of the Hope Diamond from India is a fascinating example of this, as every owner of the royal rock was bankrupted until it was finally nestled in the safe of the Smithsonian Institution in Washington, D.C.

Diamonds are associated with lightning and ensuring victory for the warriors who wore them. They are thought to be powerful enough to repel madness and even to stave off the devil himself! The medieval mystic Rabbi Benoni believed that diamonds were conducive to true spiritual joy and had power over the stars and planets in the heavens.

THOR'S DIAMOND LIGHTNING SPELL

Gather Together

Outdoor altar or small table (you can even use a large stool)

Dark blue cloth

Small hammer

1 blue candle

1 silver candle

Small stone from your backyard or neighborhood

Diamonds or Herkimer diamonds (fine if set in jewelry like a ring or earrings)

Silver-colored dish for the diamonds

Small, blue dish for the pieces of stone

Matches

Lavender incense stick

Chair or stool

I wore Herkimer diamond earrings while writing this book, as they are a diamond I can afford. They are lovely, clear crystals which are rare in that they are only found in one place on Earth: Herkimer, in New York State, in the US. They inspired me to create this spell, which is intended to bring the magic of the stars and sky into your life.

At midnight, go outside with all your ritual materials and set up your altar. Cover the altar with the cloth and set the hammer in front of the two candles, along with the small stone. Say aloud the following prayer to the Norse god Thor:

God of light,

God of night,

Bring your power.

Bring it forth in this midnight hour.

Now place the diamonds in the silver dish at the front of your altar. Light the candles, then the incense, and pass the smoke over the hammer, stone, and diamonds.

Place the stone on the ground. Pick up the hammer and say:

With this hammer, I invoke Thor's power—lightning and thunder.

On this night, I am imbued with the energy of the stars and sky!

On this night, the energy of the stars enters these diamonds from the sky.

From now on, this magic is with me and can't be put asunder.

And so it is!

Take the hammer and strike the stone, which will cause a dust of sparks, representing the great Norse god's power. They are not always visible, but they are there. The stone might break, but simply gather up the pieces and place them in the blue dish. Sit on the chair or stool for an hour and take in the power of the moment. When you need strength in your life, this spell will help.

Wearing the jewelry or crystals that you imbued with Thor's power will increase your own personal power and give you a feeling of being centered.

EARTH AND WATER STONE SPELL

Gather Together

Outdoor altar or small table (you can even use a large stool)

White cloth or scarf

2 white pillar candles

Small, white bowl half-filled with water

2 white roses

White sage leaves

2 small, white stones (either moonstones or stones found in your neighborhood)

Fireproof dish or abalone shell

Matches

Any white stone will suffice for this spell, but moonstones are the optimal crystal to use. Moonstones, like opals, contain water and so represent two elements in one: water and. earth This spell will help you become grounded and provide you with emotional support.

Go outside with all the spell materials to set up your altar. Drape the cloth or scarf over the altar, then place the candles at the back and the bowl of water in the very center. Place the roses at the front and the sage on the right. Put the two stones in the bowl of water. Light the candles, then the sage leaves with one of the candle flames. Reach into the bowl to pick up the stones and, holding one in each hand, say aloud:

Stone of Water and Earth,

Bring me grounding and calm.

Stone of Earth and Water,

I feel your power in my palm.

Upset and woe, leave me now.

Worry and sorry is gone from me now.

And so it is!

Repeat the spell twice and then extinguish the candles and the sage leaves in the water bowl. Put the roses in the bowl, then place this on the main altar inside your home along with the candles and the stones. Leave everything in place for at least two days and a sense of comfort and calm should imbue your home.

This spell is ideal during a waxing moon but can be of great use any time you need serenity or to keep worry and woe at bay.

Calcite: Bones of the Earth

The ancients believed that calcite placed at the base of a pyramid could amplify its power. The Bosporus, one of the first sites where calcite was mined and gathered, was also raided early on by Gothic tribes and then later by the Huns, led by the legendary chief Attila. After discovering the healing power of calcite, the Celts collected this stone, which was often to be found in caves. It strengthens the bones and functions as an aid to psychics. For the magical folk of today, calcite provides a powerful boost to psychism—for example, it can be worn during tarot readings for greater intuition.

Work with calcite Remarkably, calcite can be used to increase intelligence and clarify the emotions at the same time. If a relationship or work situation is confusing, and you don't understand another person's intentions or behavior, meditation with calcite will clear that difficulty up and give you complete transparency.

Lapis Lazuli: The Listening Stone

The wise old healers relied on this beautiful blue crystal so much that they ground it up to use in tiny quantities in potions. Lapis lazuli is very nearly second to none as a thought amplifier. It also enhances psychic power and can open the Third Eye chakra when laid very briefly on the forehead over the Third Eye. Nowadays, almost all of us are overextended and become so busy that we move away from our core. There is a danger in this, as we can move off-track and stop living our lives—instead, our lives end up living us. We can get so caught up in the business of work and home and family obligations that we are not living out our destinies. Lapis lazuli stone will help you stay in touch with your essence, with who you are supposed to become. Lapis lazuli is a guide to be listened to in absolute stillness. In today's world of endless distraction, this blue gem will help you regain your balance—blue is always the color of peace, spirituality, and tranquility. It is such a powerful healer of the mind and spirit. Wear it for mindfulness and to achieve a sense of wellbeing.

LAPIS LAZULI MEDITATION FOR MIND AND BODY

Gather Together

Blue candle

Lapis lazuli crystal

Matches

Dive deep into lapis lazuli's blue pool of positive energy when you feel the need to sharpen your mind or if you are feeling worn down and overburdened.

Light the candle and hold the crystal in front of your eyes so you can see the light of the flame gleaming slightly through the stone. Pray aloud:

A quickening runs through me,

I feel the beat of my heart this day.

My soul, body, and mind are as one.

*I am whole and hale today
and all tomorrows.*

And so it is. Blessed be me.

Repeat the spell three times, then extinguish the candle and place the lapis lazuli crystal on your altar. Keep it there for a while for those times you need a pick-me-up.

LITHOMANCY: CRYSTALLINE FORTUNES

Gather Together

12 small crystals or gems in a drawstring cloth bag

Soft, white cloth cut into a circle, 12 inches (30 cm) in diameter

Pad of paper and pen for writing questions and notes

People have been using stones to tell fortunes and the future since the time of the earliest humans. Rocks were not only useful as tools and for holding heat from fires, but small, beautiful, colored stones were also considered to be lucky. Many burial sites and archeological digs from the Paleolithic Period (the Old Stone Age), have revealed that rocks, gems, and crystals were used as ritual objects and clearly viewed as sacred enough to take to the next life. Perhaps a form of the crystal divination described below was used at cave-side campfires during the more recent Bronze Age (3000–1000 BCE)!

While you organize the setup for your lithomancy reading, ponder the questions currently on your mind—perhaps regarding a romantic relationship, your job, health considerations, friendship, your home, or other matters. Write your questions in the pad.

For example, if your question is about love: Ask your question, then take three of the crystals from the bag and toss them onto the cloth. Note the position they land in. The stone that's closest to the center of the cloth symbolizes your action, true feelings, or motivation for asking. The crystal second closest to the center represents the person you are interested in, as well as their feelings, motivations, and passions, and the crystal closest to the outside of the circle signifies an unseen force or outside perspective.

Now it's time to uncover what each crystal represents for you. Think of the qualities each crystal traditionally represents—for example, rose quartz means self-love; ruby represents passion; and amethyst is for healing. Hold each crystal to your heart, one at a time, and ask it to reveal a message for you. Close your eyes and clear your mind, then allow emotions, symbols, images, words, and ideas to flow freely through your mind.

When you feel that you've identified the meaning of each crystal, pause and note down what you think the message is and whatever wisdom or action you can take from it.

Repeat this for each of the three crystals. Then hold all three of them in your hand against your heart and see what their combined energy reveals. Again, write this down. There you go—you have just practiced lithomancy.

MOONSTONE MIRROR RITE

Moonstone is a psychic mirror, especially for females. The wise women of ancient times were the first to work this out. If you are feeling out-of-sorts or off-center, turn to this lovely stone, which is sacred to the shining orb in the night sky. Gaze at the moon on a moonlit night, then at your smooth, round moonstone, and look for the answer to your personal mystery. A message will come to you in the form of a dream that night.

Swift and Simple Crystal Rituals for Natural Healing

Crystals are not only a beautiful product of nature that are great for jewelry and decoration, but they are also filled with positive energy and have been used for healing and magic across the globe for centuries. If you are a beginner at witchcraft, they might seem a bit bewildering and whimsical to you, especially if you have seen complex crystal grids or the massive crystal collections amassed by other witches. That may well be your end goal, but you need not feel overwhelmed by the startling number of different crystals and their properties or the never-ending possibilities of crystal magic. At its heart, crystal magic is quite simple, and I have included some practical rituals in this section that are ideal for seasoned and beginner witches alike.

Crystals each have unique vibrational energies, which you can use to connect yourself to the Earth and are associated with a vast spectrum of healing properties. One of the fundamentals of crystal magic is intention—a crystal can be programmed with your intentions and desires and will in turn magnify your intent and assist you in bringing forth whatever sorts of changes or benefits you are seeking. It is always best to do your research and find crystals whose inherent properties complement the intention you want to focus on.

Once you have acquired and cleansed the crystal you feel is right for you in your time of need, you can begin to use it to manifest good things in your life. You might simply decorate your home with crystals or carry them around with you (as a Pisces, I like to keep stones associated with my sign, such as amethyst, on my person when I am out and about). However, incorporating them into rituals adds a fresh layer of mysticism to your life that will guide you to an even deeper connection with your spirituality. Rituals provide the practitioner with an opportunity to put a more focused intention out into the universe, and they will also be of great benefit to your mental health. Rituals are between you and the Earth, allowing you a moment, however lengthy or brief, to be alone with yourself and the powers that be.

If you are a creative busybody like me, just the idea of setting aside the time for ritual might sound tedious. We live in a very hectic, go-go-go culture, and sometimes "the grind" makes it difficult for us to work on our spiritual lives. That is what makes these rituals so perfect: they are delightfully easy and will take no more than a few minutes of your dearly precious time.

There and Back Again: A Ritual for Clarity

For this ritual, you will need: Clear quartz

Quartz is the most common mineral found on the planet, and it is also excellent for putting things into perspective. Clear quartz, with its glassy sheen, can illuminate the path before you and help you better understand your desires. It will allow you to see with more clarity the circumstances that have brought you to where you are and the direction in which you are headed.

Meditate with your quartz crystal for a minute, or for as long as you like, considering what it is that you want and how you can make your desires become reality. As you meditate, this crystal will be there to guide your understanding.

CLEANSING AND CHARGING YOUR CRYSTALS

All stones possess natural energies of their very own. You want to merge your energies with those of your crystals so that the crystals will be in sync with your vibratory channel. You can do this by cleansing your crystals and then charging them with your own energy. Remain mindful of the great power your stones have and you will be in a good position to work with it.

To cleanse your crystal, place it in a bowl of sea salt overnight and then leave it in the light of the sun for a day, making sure it is not in direct sunlight so as not to create a fire hazard. You can also surround the crystal with sage leaves, the same kind you would use for smudging (see page 21), and leave them overnight.

Once this is complete, sit in a comfortable position and hold the crystal in your right hand. Focus on the energy you desire your crystal to hold and project it into the stone. Consider carefully what kind of energy you want to place into your crystal. Bear in mind, the use of crystal magic should not be used solely for your purposes, but also for the greater good. Please make sure you're projecting positive energy and not anger or hatred. You should ask aloud for your crystal to work together with you for the highest good. You are doing creative visualization here, so keep concentrating until you can see and feel the energy flowing into the stone. You will feel when the charging, or programming, is complete; your intuition will tell you.

Freya's Love Beads Meditation

For this ritual, you will need: Rose quartz beads

Freya is a many-faceted goddess: mother, protector, wife, lover, and healer, but she is akin to Venus, the goddess of love, in many ways. A string of rose quartz prayer beads can imbue your life with romance and essential self-love. This lovely pink mineral is the stone of unconditional love and will instantly attract love from yourself and others. Rose quartz will open your heart to giving and receiving the bounties of love—self-love, familial love, romantic love, or whatever it is that you wish to manifest in your life. It can be used in a short string of a dozen beads or even as a bracelet.

Take your rose quartz string of beads and rest it against your heart as you meditate for just a few minutes on its properties and the love that you want to give and receive. Close your eyes and speak loving words and affirmations to yourself or repeat an incantation such as this: "Loving kindness flows from me. Love to myself, and love to all. So mote it be." The words can vary depending on your intentions. Let the loving energy of the rose quartz fill you and embolden you to love wildly and fearlessly.

Slay Your Daily Dragons: A Refresh Ritual to Boost Your Enthusiasm

For this ritual, you will need: Red jasper

A Norse legend has it that the great dragon-slayer Siegfried was able to handle the mighty winged beast because of the red jasper in his shield. And yes! This pretty scarlet stone can help you greet each day with greater personal power. This ritual is best performed at the beginning of the week, or any time you need an extra burst of motivation. Red jasper is an excellent stone for relieving stress and to help you ground yourself. Let this stone unleash your inner warrior, giving you the endurance that you need to get through the day, week, or difficult task that has been getting you down.

Take the red jasper stone in your hand and focus on its energies. For one minute, contemplate areas of your life where you feel you need a little extra motivation to pull through. Perhaps it's just another Monday, or you're feeling bogged down with work, or a creative block is preventing you from moving forward with your goals. While you have that situation in mind, allow a feeling of encouragement from the jasper to fill you. Know that you are not alone and that a warrior lives within you, ready to take charge in your life.

Set It in Stone: Healthy Habits Ritual

For this ritual, you will need: Blue apatite

Our northern forefolk had to deal with the gloom that comes from weeks and months with little sunlight. This sky-blue stone can send blue moods and negativity away and help you maintain a healthy, day-to-day attitude. Blue apatite rules over willpower, affecting your resolve and inspiring you to create and sustain positive change in your life. If you have ever struggled to keep your New Year's exercise, self-care, or healthy-eating resolutions, this ritual is exactly what you need. Start with just one goal that you wish to focus on to improve your health. Maybe that goal is going for a walk every other day or drinking your eight daily cups of water.

Whatever your goal, let that be your intention as you hold the crystal in your palm. Focus on the motivational power of the blue apatite and allow it to create a determined spirit within you and help you believe in your ability to achieve your health goals. From this moment on, keep the crystal close to you, and let it serve as a reminder of your goal and your promise to yourself.

Elven Energy Enchantment: Relaxation Ritual

For this ritual, you will need: Amethyst

In J. R. R. Tolkien's magical Middle Earth, the Elves wore crystal rings, including the prettiest of purple amethysts. Elves are known for their calm self-possession as well as their brilliant minds and connection to the earth, and to forests in particular. Whenever you're feeling tense or just need a little pick-me-up after a long day, amethyst is a great stone to have at hand. It is known for being the perfect crystal to promote restfulness, bring peace of mind, and calm anxiety. Its purple hue is soothing to the eye and mind, and the energy of the crystal will loosen tension in your body and help you leave the hustle and bustle of the day behind. If you have a favorite tree in your backyard or neighborhood, use this as your serenity station—there you can regain the feeling of being centered enjoyed by the tree-loving Elves.

This is another incredibly simple ritual. All you need do is visit your familiar tree and place your amethyst over the center of your forehead—your Third Eye chakra—to get in touch with the crystal's peaceful energy. Surrender all your cares and let your body be filled with the quiet vibrations of the amethyst.

Tyr's Tranquility Rite: Banish Stress and Embrace Your Zen

For this ritual, you will need: Smoky topaz

Tyr, the god for whom Tuesdays are named, ensures justice, fairness, and balance (see page 42). Invoking him can help you maintain equilibrium on a daily basis. Our busy culture produces a lot of stress in our lives. Work, school, and travel can be a constant drain on our energy levels and at the same time bog our minds down with fear and worry that we're never getting enough done. When you're stuck at the center of a workplace conflict, have a growing to-do list that is making you frantic, or are just experiencing general stress, a little magic can make a big difference. When meditating with smoky topaz, imagine that you are holding the very energy of the sun in your hands—warm, healing, and benevolent. If you are tapped out, burned-out, and at your lowest ebb, topaz will generate rays of replenishment to recharge you and get you back up to a good energy level. Smoky topaz relaxes while also replenishing you.

For this ritual, you will need two smoky topaz stones—one for each hand. Seat yourself in a comfortable position and hold the stones gently, feeling their weight on your palms, and envision them collecting pure, soothing light. Concentrate on that light as you meditate, pondering the potential for relaxation and healing that these crystals hold. Imagine that light seeping into your palms and flowing up your arms, making its way through your entire body. You will feel a wave of calm come over you as you enter a relaxed state. As you continue your day, you will be able to face the stressors that come your way from a new perspective.

Magnetic Money Magic: Conjuring Loki's Luck for Attracting Wealth

For this ritual, you will need: Pyrite

This shiny stone impresses every time you see it with its gleam and visual trick—it really does look like precious gold, hence its other name of "fool's gold." However, it does have the power to bring prosperity into your life. This trickster stone is associated with the mischief-maker Norse god Loki, who can be called on to attract money to you. Pyrite may not be especially valuable on its own, but its metallic golden shimmer makes it an excellent ritual tool for improving your finances.

To attract the energy of abundance and prosperity, lay the pyrite on top of something that you associate with money or success. This could be a literal wad of cash, a business card, or your savings jar, for example. Focus your intentions on what you are hoping to receive and invite this energy into your life. Loki is a messenger god, so write him a note, politely making your request. It can be as simple as: "Please bring me wealth [state here how you want this to manifest itself]." Be as specific as possible and state the amount, the timing, and so forth. Express full gratitude to Loki for his generosity, as you certainly want to stay on this mischievous god's good side! You may also carry this stone with you to work or a job interview for a little extra luck!

Elemental Inspiration: Amberella's Creativity Ritual

For this ritual, you will need: Amber

How wonderful is it that there is a northern European goddess named Amberella whose sacred stone is none other than amber? She is an elemental deity and connected with waters, rivers, and oceans. Amber crystal is most strongly associated with creativity, inspiration, and motivation. When I am stuck in a creative slump, this is the crystal I turn to time and again to channel and attune myself to the energy of creativity, which comes from achieving flow, a state akin to the fluidity of the element of water. This simple ritual is the perfect treatment for writer's block, coming up with ideas for the next board meeting, or for facilitating progress on a forthcoming project.

Clasp the amber between your palms and feel its vibrant energy as it absorbs the warmth of your hands. Close your eyes and then claim its creative energy for yourself. Invoke the goddess Amberella:

Goddess of the waters, ancient Amberella,

I look to your springs and font of creativity.

Thanks to you, new ideas flow from me like a river.

I have cleared away any dams slowing its flow.

So mote it be and thanks to thee.

Keep the amber with you throughout the day, so it can continue to amplify the creativity you already hold inside you.

Resting Under the Care of Nerthus:
A Celestial Slumber Crystal

For this ritual, you will need: Blue lace agate

We all slept in our mother's arms and under the loving care of a maternal presence in our early years. A mother's love can still be invoked for a good night's sleep. You can invoke the Norse goddess Nerthus, whose power crystal is blue lace agate. When you feel weary or mentally drained, try this sweet ritual, which is perfect for the everyday insomniac. We have all been there—long nights spent scrolling through social media or web articles, as we wait for exhaustion to creep in and take us, finally, to the realm of dreams. Even when we know that the blue light effect from our screens is self-defeating, keeping us awake even longer! Much better than a late-night "doom-scroll" is picking up a book, meditating, or, better yet, trying this little ritual to prepare your mind for slumber.

Place a blue lace agate between your palms before going to sleep. It will empty your mind and fill your bedroom with a restful energy to lull you to sleep. Breathe slowly and deeply, letting your eyes flutter shut. When you feel a calm beginning to settle over you, whisper to yourself: "Nerthus, goddess of night and mother to us all, give me deep sleep. On this night I shall slip into blissful slumber. In gratitude to you, blessed be." Then place the stone under your pillow or beside your bed and prepare yourself for a long, deep sleep.

Become a Stone Seer: Crystal Divination

We have already learned how the Norse people used runes for divination (see page 12), but crystals are also an excellent tool for this. If you are expecting a direct answer to your questions from divining with crystals, you may be dissatisfied, but they are wonderful when you are stuck in a sticky situation and seeking to gain clarity regarding your quandary! Keep your mind and heart open and try this dazzling divination method for yourself.

The first step in this divination practice is to procure a bag for your crystals. This bag can be something meaningful for you, but it could also be any repurposed container that will hide the crystals from view. I recommend using something that is pleasing to your eye, such as a silken satchel or velvety drawstring pouch—perhaps even one made of a selenite-infused fabric—purchased from your local metaphysical store. Once you have placed your crystals inside the bag, you are ready to begin.

Take out a single crystal. You need to make a mental note of its color, or jot this down on a piece of paper. Put the crystal back in the bag, and then draw out a second crystal. Again, write down the color and then put the crystal back in the bag. Repeat this process one more time until you have retrieved a total of three crystals.

First crystal: The first of the three crystals is indicative of the issue at hand. It may draw your attention to an existing problem, or perhaps bring to the surface an underlying matter that you may not have been consciously aware of.

Second crystal: This crystal is antagonistic and represents something that may be preventing you from reaching a solution.

Third crystal: The final crystal shows where you will find your solution—the key to regaining your peace of mind!

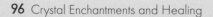

Here are some examples of the issues and answers that the various crystals might point you toward:

Red stones

(garnet, ruby, jasper, jade, bloodstone)

First stone: You might be feeling frustrated about something that is occurring in your life.

Second stone: There are likely many strong emotions involved in the issue at hand, which may be a source of hostility.

Third stone: You will find a solution to your troubles by transforming negative emotions from yourself or other involved individuals into something more constructive; translate anger into affirmative action rather than letting it simmer.

Pink stones

(topaz, rose quartz, rhodochrosite)

First stone: Perhaps your conflict lies in the divide between following your heart, and pursuing what is right for you, and doing what is best for the world at large.

Second stone: Your own sense of self-importance and your material desires are distracting you.

Third stone: Treat everyone you meet with love as though they are dear to your heart, even if they are strangers to you.

Purple stones

(amethyst, fluorite, lepidolite)

First stone: There may be some disruption in your life caused by an imbalance between your earthly life and your spirituality.

Second stone: You are letting minor concerns and trials divert your attention from what truly matters to you.

Third stone: When difficulties come your way, take them in your stride. Allow a sense of calm to fill you as you remember that your struggles will pass and be forgotten in light of the grander scheme of things.

Blue stones

(aquamarine, lapis lazuli, sapphire)

First stone: You may be facing a dilemma as to whether you should say what's on your mind or leave things to chance.

Second stone: The people in your life will take advantage of you if you do not stand up for yourself or make your voice heard. Your quiet will become their permission.

Third stone: Be honest and speak without fear. When the truth comes out, justice will take its due course.

Green stones

(malachite, jade, aventurine)

First stone: Perhaps you are facing a situation where you need to decide whether to follow the whims and longings of your heart or sacrifice your own wellbeing for the sake of someone else.

Second stone: There is a possibility that your loving soul has put you in a position to be used by others who would emotionally manipulate you for their own purposes.

Third stone: Listen to what your instinct tells you. You need to trust yourself more, and give of yourself only if it feels right, not because of any outside influence. You will know what the right choice is.

Yellow stones

(citrine, jasper, honey calcite)

First stone: You are trying to be in too many places and do too many things at once.

Second stone: Though you may put time and dedication into what you do, your endeavors are being sabotaged. At the root of the problem lies deceit and envy.

Third stone: Be mindful of the things that the people in your life have to say about you. Some of them may be more accurate than you care to admit, regardless of whether those things are positive or negative. Keep your priorities in order.

Orange stones

(sunstone, amber, carnelian)

First stone: You may find that your emotional needs are being neglected. Alternatively, there is a chance that you are not staying true to yourself and what you believe in some facet of your life.

Second stone: There may be someone overstepping their boundaries and exerting their influence and control over you. You may be blissfully unaware of this, especially if that person is being subtle in the way they've been overshadowing you.

Third stone: Be kind and firm as you enforce your boundaries. You need to stand up for yourself and what you deserve, but this does not need to be at the expense of anyone else's self-image.

Black stones

(obsidian, tourmaline, onyx)

First stone: You have quite a few affairs in your life that have been left unsettled.

Second stone: You are trapped in a position that is detrimental to you, but your own worries and insecurities are keeping you there.

Third stone: The best way to solve your dilemma is by using acts of kindness and love to negate harmful energies and destructive frames of mind.

White stones

(moonstone, howlite, selenite)

First stone: It's possible that you are feeling discontented with the way you are living and want to make some sort of significant change.

Second stone: The idea of change makes you anxious as it may threaten to upset the lifestyle you've grown comfortable with.

Third stone: Now is the time to set changes in motion. Be gentle with yourself as you transition into new experiences and phases of life and release your fear of the unknown.

Gray stones

(smoky quartz, labradorite, moonstone)

First stone: You're stuck in a liminal space between clinging to the past and moving on.

Second stone: It may be that uncertainty is preventing you from realizing your potential. Doubt on your part or that of someone closely involved in your life is becoming too pervasive.

Third stone: Find resolution in knowing that nothing in life is ever truly black and white, and this includes the issues that trouble you. The gray space in between is what gives you the freedom to make your own way.

PROTECTION MAGIC: DIY AMULETS

Amulets are protective adornments that date back to the beginning of human civilization. They are magical jewelry and the Norse employed them daily, often carving runes on them, directly into the stones and metal. When traveling, they would wear amulets, believing they could guide them if they got lost and keep them safe on the road. Amulets carved with a symbol of the sun, representing the god Thor (see page 43), were considered very lucky. Evil eye amulets are perhaps the most globally popular, believed in most cultures to be capable of warding off a hex by reflecting it back to its origins. In some cultures, amulets were devoted to a specific god or goddess, and it was thought the wearer would be protected by that divinity. You can make your own amulets for yourself or friends. First, you must select a crystal associated with the energy you wish to manifest:

Aventurine: Shows new horizons are ahead

Ruby: Helps you dare for deep passion and personal power

Emerald: Brings prosperity

Sapphire: Means you will know the truth

Hematite: Provides abundance and groundedness

Snowflake obsidian: Keeps troubles at bay

Hold the crystal in your hand until it gets warm, then visualize the specific power the stone is offering. If the amulet is for you, wear it as a pendant or tuck it in your pocket.

Chapter 5

TRANSFORMATIVE ESSENCES AND INCENSE

In the cold climes where the Norse people lived, creating comfort
was key. Achieve a feeling of coziness in your own home with these
natural soothing scents and herbal teas.

Sanctuary and Sacredness

The last time I celebrated the Winter Solstice (December 21) and Yule (see page 124) at my home here in the US, my honored guest commented that the space felt like a sanctuary and safe haven. I was, of course, delighted to hear this and asked for further explanation. He answered that the moment you walk into my home, there is a scent of the sacred, from the candles, incense, potpourris, and even the occasional hearth fires burning Palo Santo, other fragrant woods and branches, and cinnamon. He said there was a feeling of being on holy ground. I thought about his comment later and realized that this homeliness, or *hygge* as the Scandinavians call it, is the culmination of years of effort, a certain mindfulness and attention to what elements to bring into my personal spaces, as well as, very importantly, the intention behind them.

I have incorporated everything I have learned from the wise women in my family and the greater community to which I belong into my mindfulness regarding home and the creation of sacred spaces. I count myself very lucky to have learned from, widely read, and studied under John Michael Greer, the Arch Druid himself, as well as Diana Paxson, one of the preeminent scholars of the Norse ways, both of whom have made many pilgrimages to northern Europe, Iceland, and even Arctic lands. I also love eastern and northern Europe and intend to spend a lot more time there, relaxing and picking up new wisdom. I love the fact that those places in which it seems quite a challenge to create hygge, or a sense of cozy homeliness, are the very same locations that the heart and hearth of this feeling come from!

Once I learned the art of *hygge*, creating comfort and coziness in my personal space, I fell under the spell of the practice and set about creating charms and enchantments that tap into this special kind of magic. Here, I share my trademark recipes for incenses, potions, potpourris, teas, and all kinds of comforts gathered from my family and created by my own hand. Scent is a large part of these recipes and the main reason why you can walk into my temple space and immediately feel safe and secure in a sanctuary intended to offer deep comfort and a sense of being surrounded by holiness.

GODDESS OF LIGHT AND DARKNESS BLESSING BREW

Gather Together

2–3 quarts (2–3 liters) water

Large flameproof pot (with a capacity of at least 3 quarts/3 liters)

1 blood orange, sliced

1 large apple, sliced

⅓ cup (35 g) fresh cranberries

6 broken cinnamon sticks

2 whole vanilla beans (pods)

1 tablespoon whole cloves

¼ teaspoon ground nutmeg

Handful of rosemary sprigs

Wooden spoon

½ cup (70 g) fresh pomegranate seeds

Airtight container for storing the brew (optional)

We all remember from high school mythology that the seeds of the pomegranate were part of the legend of why the Greek demi-goddess Persephone lived half the year below and half the year above ground—by eating pomegranate seeds, she bound herself irrevocably to Hades, the god of the underworld. Pomegranate is one of the most holy of fruits. Not only does it look and taste delicious, but it can also add a very sacred dimension to this stovetop potpourri brew:

Warm 2 quarts (2 liters) of the water in the pot over a very gentle heat on the stovetop and add the sliced fruits and cranberries, then stir in all the spices and the rosemary with the wooden spoon. Add the pomegranate seeds last and stir them in gently. Within half an hour, an amazing aroma should begin wafting around the kitchen. I keep the mixture at a low simmer for a few hours and add more water over time. The finished drink should have the consistency of mulled wine. Strain, pour, and serve. I also like to keep the finished brew in a lidded container in the refrigerator and then re-steep it in a little water before drinking when I need some goddess energy and goddess-blessings!

PEACE OF MIND POTPOURRI

Gather Together

Large baking sheet

2 large sheets of parchment paper

3-4 oranges, thinly sliced

3 cups (340 g) fresh cranberries

8-10 chestnuts

3 ounces (85 g) whole cloves

3 ounces (85 g) star anise

3 ounces (85 g) whole nutmeg

2 ounces (60 g) juniper berries

1 ounce (28 g) whole allspice

12 cinnamon sticks

Large ceramic bowl

Wooden spoon

4 drops clove essential oil

4 drops vanilla essential oil

4 drops cinnamon essential oil

The very act of creating this fragrant mix will create calm in your day while filling your home or workspace with natural perfumes. The spices, berries, and oranges are easy to source in your local neighborhood and it is lovely to keep this potpourri on your altar or wherever you want the spicy and sweet scents to abound.

Preheat the oven to 300°F (150°C/Gas 2) and line the baking sheet with parchment paper. Spread the orange slices, cranberries, and chestnuts over the paper. Bake in the oven for 4 to 6 hours or until everything is completely dry.

Add all the spices to the bowl, stirring them in one at a time. Lastly, add the essential oils to the bowl and stir everything clockwise four times, as you say aloud:

As I create this feeling

And the space for healing,

All is peaceful and bright,

All is surrounded by light.

May all be well in this space.

May all be filled with divine grace.

So mote it be.

This magical mixture will imbue your space with lovely vibrations and infuse your life with tranquility.

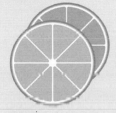

MAGICAL CORRESPONDENCES

- **Oranges** are associated with happiness in love.
- **Chestnuts** are connected to love and higher consciousness.
- **Juniper berries** help with warding off unkind thoughts and adverse energies.
- **Cranberries** are good for healing as well as for protection, love, and positive energy.

Idun, Wild Apple Goddess of Youth and Beauty

We know from the history and lore of the era that the Vikings made the most of the abundance of local nuts and berries, including raspberries, blueberries, lingonberries, bilberries, and so forth, as well as wild plums and apples. They regarded the apple as being particularly hallowed. Being connected to Idun, the little-known pastoral goddess of Norse mythology, the hardy Vikings knew that apples kept them healthy. It was also believed that the beneficence of Idun gave the gift of youthfulness through her consecrated fruit, the apple, and so she became known as "The Rejuvenating One." Even gods and goddesses depended on apples for their eternally youthful and beautiful appearances.

APPLES OF IMMORTALITY LOVE SPELL

Gather Together

2 cups (480 ml) apple cider vinegar

2 cups (480 ml) warm water

Towel

Apple essential oil for anointing

Glass of apple juice

2 large red apples

Idun is the harbinger of spring and not only holds sway over apples, but also poetry. Invoking Idun with this spell will restore or highlight the glow of beauty and youth and help you attract love.

Wash your hands and face in the apple cider vinegar diluted in the bowl of warm water (the vinegar is caustic to the skin, so always dilute before using). Once you're toweled dry, anoint yourself with some apple essential oil on pulse points such as the wrists, neck, and over the heart. Drink from the glass of apple juice and say this spell aloud:

Idun, goddess of immortality,
I call upon thou.

Send the flower of youth to me now.

I take the gift of your apple from
this bough

And will return the gift of my love, I vow.

And so it is. Blessed be thou.

Now take up one of the apples and eat it. Place the other apple on your altar for a full day and night. You will look fresher and more attractive to others, and love will come to you soon.

Incense to Instill Your Life with Magic

To invoke the energy of the Norse gods in your household, I recommend lighting some incense that correlates with their powers and personalities. Here is a list of a few prominent gods and goddesses, along with suitable incenses that you can buy online or at your local spiritual store.

Thor The god of thunder, strength, and protection, Thor can give you the power and courage to face down the bullies in your life and achieve your goals. If you are seeking Thor's protection and guidance, try lighting some amber, oak, or valerian incense.

Freya The goddess of love, fertility, battle, and death, Freya is as lovely as she is fierce, and is also considered a *völva* (a female shaman and seeress in Norse culture—see page 53), because she introduced the gods to the art of seidr (or divination). To draw in the energy of Divine Feminine power and attract new love and desire, light some jasmine or rose incense.

Bragi If you are suffering from a creative block, turn to Bragi, the wise bard and god of poetry, for help. Light sandalwood incense to fill your space with the inspiration and creative potential of this divine poet.

Heimdall Heimdall is the vigilant protector of the realm of the gods and will help you to spot and avoid dangers along your path. For insight, increased awareness, and protection, burn sandalwood or birch incense to attract the energy of Heimdall.

Eir A lesser goddess of healing and possibly a Valkyrie (see page 36), Eir was said to have been a skilled physician, so if you are in need of a little healing, try burning myrrh or juniper incense to receive strength from this heavenly healer.

Freyr The god of peace, prosperity, and fertility, Freyr is also associated with sunshine and will attract financial success and abundance to your home. To invite in the energy of prosperity from Freyr, light mint, rose, or sandalwood incense.

Baldur Baldur is the god of love, beauty, light, and rebirth. He is known for his radiant beauty, fairness, and honesty. Seek his favor when you desire to birth new things in your life, such as new love or positive habits, or when you feel you need a little burst of joy in your day. The best incense to evoke the essence of the god Baldur is cinnamon or frankincense.

Mimir Mimir is the god of peace, knowledge, and wisdom. Meditating with some cinnamon, eucalyptus, or sandalwood incense will help you clear your mind and find a solution to your most pressing issues with Mimir's guidance. You may also find that his essence brings you a feeling of calm, dissipating tension and anxiety.

Frigga Known as Frigga or Frigg, the wife of Odin is associated with marriage, motherhood, the home, and clairvoyance. Like Freya, she too was a seeress, and her energy can assist you in your divination practice and fill your home with a sense of familial comfort and safety. For Frigga's guidance, burn cedar or mistletoe incense.

Odin The god of wisdom and war, Odin is one of the major figures of Norse mythology. If you are facing an imminent struggle, need a boost of confidence, or seeking wisdom to guide you through a difficult situation, try lighting some nag champa (a blend of sandalwood and either champak or frangipani) or juniper incense to receive Odin's insight.

SANCTUARY SALVE:
DIY SELF-CARE BLEND

Gather Together

6 tablespoons walnut oil

2 tablespoons apricot oil

25 drops lemon balm essential oil

5 drops balsam essential oil

3 drops cedar essential oil

Medium-size, dark blue bottle with a stopper

With this marvelous blend of oils, you can beckon the energies of forest water and earth and combine these with the spirit of health and positivity in your day. Walnut, apricot, lemon balm, balsam, and cedar oils create a delightful and sensory scent that lingers on your skin for hours.

Add the walnut and apricot oils and essentials oils to the bottle, put on the lid (ensure that this fits tightly), and shake well to combine. You now have serenity in a bottle that you can dab on your skin, as required.

Note: Aromatherapy using flower and herbal essences can also be used in diffusers to infuse the air with your preferred fragrance. Many of the most heady and powerful essential oils blend well together. Try a combination of amber and apple, ylang ylang and sandalwood, clary sage and rose, or almond and neroli. If you're using a candle diffuser, then rose or orange blossom water makes an aromatic and romantic alternative to plain water in the diffuser cup.

QUICK QUIETUDE: AROMATHERAPY SPA SCENTS

Lavender Love

The lovely colors and sweet overtones of perfume make lavender a well-known plant in many homes. One thick bunch of dried lavender will fill your home with a lasting, calming scent for a relaxing, spa-like atmosphere. I keep a bowl of lavender seeds in my bathroom and every time I shower or bathe, the superb scent fills the room, adding calm and clarity to my day.

Eucalyptus Energy

There are few scents as amazing for your space as silver dollar eucalyptus (*Eucalyptus cinerea*)—the menthol fragrance lingers long after the branches have begun to dry out. Place the branches in your shower to fill the space with a stress-free cloud of minty fragrance. The beautiful round leaves make a gorgeous bouquet, too.

Peppermint Positivity

Delightfully aromatic peppermint has miracle magical uses and will engender an uplifting energy into your sacred space. This is an instant mood lifter! Take a palmful of dried peppermint and place it on your altar. Crush some of the dried herb in your hands and leave it there for a full day for energetic clearing and positivity.

WITCHY WICKS: THE EASY ENCHANTMENT OF CANDLES

Gather Together

Candle wick

Vessel such as a glass container for the candle

Shallow saucepan filled with 2 inches (5 cm) of cold water

Hot plate or electric stove

Shredded wax (available online and from craft stores)

Incense of your choice

2 popsicle sticks or similar to hold the wick in place

Norse folk lived in lands where it got dark very early for much of the year. In the era before the advent of electricity, they needed to create their own sources of light using candles and fire. Candle-making is one of the most practical forms of magic and involves three simple ingredients: a wick, wax, and a vessel to hold them.

Before melting the wax, place the wick in your choice of candle container. I often choose a clean, empty container previously used for a candle, as this is both eco-friendly and budget-friendly! Place the container in the saucepan of water on top of a hot plate or electric stove and set the heat to very low. Do not use the flame of a gas stove as this is too tricky to control and we want to avoid any chance of fire. Carefully add the shredded wax to the container, keeping the wick as central as you can. Let the wax melt slowly and keep adding more until the container is full.

Now, add your choice of fragrance for the desired effect. Use a couple of popsicle sticks or similiar to keep the candle wick in place—simply sandwich the wick between the two sticks laid across the top of the container. Let the wax cool completely and then trim the wick down to size.

INCENSE INSPIRATION

- **Ginger** will bring more money into your space, as well as success.
- **Cardamom** is used in love magic and will also bring you tranquility.
- **Allspice** is effective in healing work.
- **Nutmeg** awakens psychic responses and prophetic dreams.
- **Clove** is excellent for invoking protection and banishing negativity.

Flowers and Herbs of the Gods and Goddesses

Scented flowers and verdant herbs are a very direct way to connect to different divinities. You can use the energies of these plants in so many ways—in gardens, potpourris, incenses, and teas. They are available at herbalist stores or from your favorite witchy store in the form of essential oils. Below are a few plants and their divine connections:

- **Barley:** Odin
- **Bird's foot trefoil (*Lotus corniculatus*):** Olwen (Welsh sun goddess)
- **Blackthorn (*Prunus spinosa*):** The Triple Goddess (see page 38)
- **Cornflower (*Centaurea cyanus*):** Flora
- **Cowslip (*Primula veris*):** Freya
- **Daffodil (*Narcissus*):** Persephone (wife of Hades and queen of the underworld)
- **Daisy (*Bellis perennis*):** Artemis, Freya, Thor, Venus, and Zeus
- **Dandelion (*Taraxacum officinale*):** Brigid (Irish goddess of healers, poets, and childbirth)
- **Flax (*Linum usitatissimum*):** Hulda (Teutonic goddess of fertility)
- **Holly (*Ilex*):** Frau Holle (Scandinavian goddess of healing)
- **Leek:** Thor
- **Meadowsweet (*Filipendula ulmaria*):** Blodeuwedd (goddess of flowers and emotions)
- **Moss:** Tapio (Finnish god of forests)
- **Motherwort (*Leonorus cardiaca*):** All mother goddesses
- **Primrose (*Primula vulgaris*):** Freya
- **Thistles:** Thor
- **Vervain (*Verbena*):** Valkyries
- **Water lily (*Nymphaea*):** All water deities
- **Wild strawberry (*Fragaria vesca*):** Venus, Freya

Make-At-Home Hygge Teas: Blissful Brews

Hygge summarizes in a single word the exact feeling of cozying up by the fire with a warm blanket, a book, and a steaming mug of your favorite tea while you watch the rain or snow falling outside your window. The *hygge* lifestyle is an essential part of Danish culture and is all about celebrating the simple warmth of everyday life. The following tea recipes are designed to fill you with that same idyllic contentedness, both as you prepare and enjoy them! You can drink several cups of each tea by yourself, or share with a friend or partner.

BERGAMOT BLISSING BREW

Gather Together

Kettle

2 tablespoons loose-leaf Earl Grey tea

1–2 teaspoons dried lavender blossoms

Teapot strainer or tea infuser

Teapot

Small fresh mint leaf

Heatsafe mug or cup

Heavy (double) cream or milk and sugar, to taste

Earl Grey tea has long been a tea-lover's staple, but this recipe, incorporating the soothing notes of lavender with the sharpness of bergamot, brings a new dimension to an old favorite.

Start by boiling the water for your tea—a kettle is fine for this. While you are waiting for the water to boil, place the loose-leaf tea and lavender blossoms in a teapot strainer or tea infuser. Pour the hot water over the strainer or infuser in the teapot, then cover and leave to steep for five minutes. Put a mint leaf at the bottom of your mug or cup. Once the tea is ready, pour it into your mug or cup. Add cream and sugar to taste and your evening of bliss awaits!

ENCHANTMENT OF LEMON TEA: BLEND FOR THE SOUL

Gather Together

Kettle

¾ cup (30 g) dried lemongrass

¼ cup (10 g) dried lemon balm

¼ cup (10 g) dried lemon peel

¼ cup (10 g) dried chamomile

Bowl

Airtight glass jar (optional)

Teapot strainer or tea infuser

Teapot

Heatsafe mug or cup

Apple honey, to taste

This blend creates a gentle, calming tea that's good for both body and soul. In my opinion, this is best as a morning tea, as it will leave your mind feeling clear and refreshed, ready for the day ahead.

Start by boiling the water for your tea—a kettle is fine for this. Meanwhile, combine all the herbs in a bowl and mix well. I like to store my tea blends in an airtight glass jar that I can keep on a shelf in my pantry. To make a single serving of tea, you will need one teaspoon of the herb blend. Add this to the strainer or infuser in the teapot and pour over the hot water. Cover and let steep for 5 to 10 minutes. Pour the tea into your mug or cup and sweeten with apple honey.

SPICE AND FLOWER:
HEARTY ROSE CARDAMOM TEA

Gather Together

1 cup (240 ml) water

Saucepan

3 cardamom pods

4–5 dried rosebuds or ½ teaspoon rose water

1 teaspoon loose-leaf black tea

Large, fine-mesh strainer (such as a chinois)

Heatsafe mug or cup

Milk or heavy (double) cream, to taste

Sweetener of choice, to taste

Hazelnut and a nut mill

This tea is a personal favorite of mine, as it is both delicious and simple to make! The spice of the cardamom intermingles beautifully with the floral notes of the rose to create a flavor that is highly addictive.

Heat the water in a saucepan on the stovetop, bringing it to a simmer. Crush the cardamom pods and add them to the pan. Add the rosebuds or rose water next—when using dried rosebuds, I like to crush them slightly first to break the petals apart. Bring the simmering water to a boil, and then add the black tea. Boil for 1 minute and then remove from the heat, covering the pan and leaving to steep for 3 to 4 minutes. Strain the tea into your favorite mug or cup and then add milk or cream and sweetener, according to preference. Now, grind just a tiny bit of hazelnut skin into the tea to give you wisdom and inspiration.

WINTER WONDERLAND PEPPERBERRY ICED TEA

Gather Together

1 teaspoon dried peppermint leaves

1 teaspoon sugar, plus extra to sweeten

Heatsafe mug or cup

1 cup (240 ml) boiling water

1 tablespoon fresh blueberries

Ice cubes

Glass

Tea strainer

If you have a backyard, you can grow and dry your own peppermint for this tea. If you don't have a backyard, or you'd rather not have to wait while you cultivate and dry the mint, you can order dried peppermint online or try your local organic grocery store. Blueberries, beloved for their health-giving properties, add a burst of fresh flavor to the tea and give you peace and protection. I love this recipe, as it is so easy to prepare and makes for an incredibly refreshing and cozy beverage.

Put the peppermint and 1 teaspoon of sugar in the mug or cup, and then pour in the boiling water. Add the blueberries and mash them together with the peppermint and sugar, then stir in as much additional sugar as you would like, according to taste. Let the tea steep for 3 minutes. Add some ice cubes to a glass, then strain the tea over the ice for quick cooling. Drink and enjoy.

ROSEMARY MAJESTY HERBAL BLEND

Gather Together

1 ½ cups (60 g) finely crushed dried peppermint leaves

1 teaspoon finely crushed dried thyme

1 ounce (28 g) finely crushed dried rosemary

½ ounce (14 g) finely crushed dried sage leaves

Bowl

Airtight container (optional)

1 cup (240 ml) boiling water

Tea strainer

Heatsafe mug or cup

Honey, to taste

You might be surprised to find a recipe for rosemary tea, but I can guarantee you will also be surprised by how delicious this is to drink. Rosemary is also high in antioxidants and is a proven mood booster!

Combine the peppermint, thyme, rosemary, and sage in a bowl, blending them thoroughly. If you wish, you can store the herbal tea blend in an airtight container in your pantry or another cool place. To make a single serving of the tea, steep one tablespoon of the herb blend in about 1 cup (240 ml) of boiling water. You can steep the tea to taste, leaving it a short while for a milder tea and longer if you prefer a stronger flavor. Strain the tea into the mug or cup and sweeten with honey, if desired.

SOOTHING JUNIPER AND GINGER ELIXIR

Gather Together

Juice of ½ lemon

1-inch (2.5-cm) piece of fresh ginger

1 juniper berry

1 teaspoon honey

1 cup (240 ml) water

Saucepan

Large, fine-mesh strainer (such as a chinois)

Heatsafe mug or cup

This tea is an excellent choice when you need a little pick-me-up. I find it to be an excellent curative for a cold or sore throat, and its taste is blissfully comforting. Juniper brings the magic of protection, too.

Heat the lemon juice, ginger, juniper berry, honey, and water in a saucepan over a medium heat. Once the mixture is thoroughly heated, strain into a mug or cup. All that's left to do is enjoy!

CONTENTMINT TEA

Gather Together

2 cups (480 ml) water

Saucepan

4 teaspoons fennel seeds

4 teaspoons coriander seeds

2 teaspoons peppercorns

1½ teaspoons whole cumin seeds

Jar with a lid

Bowl or mortar and pestle

3 slices of fresh ginger

15 fresh mint leaves

Airtight container

Large, fine-mesh strainer
(such as a chinois)

Heatsafe mug or cup

3 lemon slices (optional)

This classic mint tea has a pleasant kick to it because of the ginger and various spices! A sip of this homemade brew will fill you with instant warmth, making it the perfect blend for a chilly day.

Begin by bringing the water to a simmer in the saucepan. While you are waiting for the water to heat, combine all the dry spices in a jar, shaking it so they are thoroughly mixed. Then, in a separate bowl, or using a mortar and pestle, pound the ginger and mint together. Once the water reaches a steady simmer, add the ginger and mint to the pan along with 1 tablespoon of the spice blend (keep the remaining blend in an airtight container in a pantry or another cool place).

Leave to simmer for about 5 minutes, then remove the pan from the heat. Cover the pan and let the tea steep for a further 3 minutes before straining into the mug or cup. I like to add the lemon slices to the strainer at this stage, straining the tea right through them, but you can also add the slices to the pan after removing it from the heat if you would like a stronger flavor.

Chapter 6

NORSE ASTROLOGY AND LUNAR LORE

The Norse year was governed by the moon and the seasons. Explore some of the traditional rituals, adapted for modern times, and their magical meanings and purposes.

Sacred Seasons of the Stars

The Germanic and Nordic pagans of old saw the year as only two seasons—winter and summer—and split it into two 26-week halves, which they kept track of by the turnings of the moon. The Old Norse words for both harvest and year were one and the same, because the years were counted by the harvests. The Old Norse word for the solar year was *Silarbangr*, and the year began at midsummer around June 21, the longest day of the year when the sun prevailed over everything. These northern European tribes began the new year at the setting of the sun, a ritual they shared with two other tribal peoples: the Celts and the Hebrews. This was followed in June by the summer feast day of Sumarmail.

Due to their proximity to the north pole, the onset of wintertime came just four months later and was celebrated with a winter night festival that involved offerings to please the gods. The Norse folk who migrated to Iceland had to adapt this schedule slightly to accommodate the even more extreme winters experienced there. Iceland was on its own specialized climatic schedule, so for Icelanders, summer began in mid-April; as a result, they celebrated Sumarmail then. Some scholars theorize that this is the true origin of Ostara—one of the eight sabbats that celebrates the spring equinox—and that it was later Christianized as Easter. The inventive Icelanders further compensated for their slightly out-of-sync seasons and calendar by adding four more days during summertime and an entire week every seven years.

Yule is one of the sabbats, or eight solar holidays, and is celebrated on December 21, the shortest day of the year. The word Yule comes from the Germanic *jol*, meaning "midwinter." It was an important festival for the Germanic and Nordic tribes and timed to coincide with the Winter Solstice. For the peoples living in Scandinavia and the extreme far north, Yule came when the sun returned to the sky after a long period of darkness.

In olden Scandinavia, most holidays and festivals took place in summertime, when people could be outside together for more than a few minutes. The Varthang, or "Spring Thing," was named for the goddess Var, who hears oaths and promises; it was a big spring celebration when important business matters were taken care of.

Legal cases were also heard and preparations made for the meeting of the assembly. The seventh week of summer, known as the Fardagar, was a time for moving into new homes and starting new tenancies, and when properties were transferred from one owner to another. Then there was the Althan, or midsummer festival. Traditions celebrated in other European areas, such as the Maypole dance, were performed with feasting and sacred rituals. Two months before the end of summertime came the Leith, or "Autumn Thing." This was the time of the Althing, the political assembly of the people. The names for the months varied from tribe to tribe and according to location. Some of the names are lost to us now, and historians theorize that the months were not named but counted instead. The winter moons were often named for the festivals.

Yule Rituals: Warming the Soul

December is named for the Roman goddess Decima, one of the Three Fates in Roman mythology. Nearly every solar god is celebrated during this month—Freyr in Nordic mythology, Bel for Syrians, Apollo for Greeks, and Osiris in Egypt, to name but a few. Scots celebrate Hogmanay in honor of their solar god, Hogmagog. Traditionally for Yule, a vigil would be held and a bonfire lit from dusk to dawn to ensure the sun did indeed rise again on this the longest night of the year.

EARTH, AIR, WATER, AND FIRE OF LIFE RITUAL

Gather Together

Sage bundle for smudging

12 candles to represent each month of the year

Matches

Bowl of salt or earth

Incense of your choice

Cup of water

1 candle to represent fire

Fireproof dish or abalone shell

Cake, cookies, or candy (sweets) to share with those gathered

This ritual is about the fire of life and how to keep it burning continuously in your own life.

Start by smudging the area with sage (see page 21). Arrange the 12 candles in a circle in the room where you are performing the ritual. Light the candles and create a sacred space by placing a symbol of each of the four elements inside the circle: a bowl of salt or earth, incense (to represent air), a cup of water, and a candle (for fire). Sit inside the circle of candles and become fully centered and completely relaxed in the flickering candlelight. Note the presence of the four elements and the balance they create. Notice how warm and alive the room feels. Notice how the gentle, flickering candlelight makes you feel safe. Now consider all the events you have experienced over the past year and think of the people in your life. Imagine them surrounded by the warm, loving candlelight, and say to each of them, one by one:

I release the past with love and understanding.

May the light of Yule bless you.

Blessed be me and thee.

As you release each person or situation, visualize their image melting into the candlelight. As the image fades from your mind's eye, place a piece of cake or other confection in your mouth. Allow the treat to dissolve, spreading its sweetness across your tongue. Visualize and feel that sweetness spreading through you, counteracting any traces of pain or bitterness that might remain. This is the sweetness that your new life holds, untainted by the bitter demons that have held you back. Say out loud:

I taste the sweetness of life and see the future bright with hope.

Stay within your circle of light for as long as you desire. Leave some of the cake, cookies, or candy as an offering to the gods in thanks for your new life.

THE GATE OF THE NEW YEAR

This year, open your home to your fellow Norse pagans who are traveling to or from celebrations, and provide them with an opportunity to pause and refresh before going on to other gatherings or returning home to their cozy beds. Prepare your space with a thorough smudging (see page 21) before they arrive.

Your wayfarers' enchanted experience begins at the threshold of your front door. Create a shrine in your home by taking three bowls and adding clean sand to one, incense to another, and fresh water to the third. Light the candle and the incense. You have now created symbols of the four elements: earth, air, water, and fire. Use the paper or cardstock to write a sign to go with your shrine that simply reads:

At the Gate of the New Year,

Purify your hands with water so you may receive peace;

Light a stick of incense so you may receive freedom;

Offer the candle, so you may receive guiding light.

Gather Together

3 large bowls

1 cup of clean sand

Incense of your choice

1 cup of fresh water

1 votive candle

Matches

Piece of paper or cardstock and a pen

During their visit, offer your guests the opportunity to divine their fortunes for the coming year with all manner of divination systems: rune readings, tarot readings, stone seeing, scrying (the practice of looking into media such as stones, crystals, glass, water, and smoke for significant messages or visions), and the I Ching. If you are not a tarotist, engage the services of a friend who is skilled in the arts of divination. This quiet oasis in an otherwise raucous day and night will provide your fellow revelers with a chance to reflect on their lives during the year that is passing away and the possibilities for the year to come—to both look backward and forward, like the two-faced Roman god Janus, the god of gates and doors, beginnings and endings.

SUMMER HARVEST MOON FESTIVAL

The harvest season celebration that takes place on the harvest moon, the full moon closest to the autumnal equinox (September 21), was especially important in days of yore when supplies had to last everyone through the winter. One lovely way to celebrate in modern times is to hold a feast that begins and ends with gratitude and blessings for the food and wine, which also includes a place setting for the great sun god.

Decorate the table as an altar with the cloth and fresh flowers and arrange chairs around it for your guests (including the sun god). Add the plates, napkins, and goblets to the altar table, along with the wine and various foods. The host should speak aloud to those gathered around the table:

*Harvest is here and the seasons
do change.*

This is the height of the year.

*The bounty of summer sustains us,
in spirit, in soul, and in body.*

*Take your seat at the table and
share the bread and bounty.*

And so it is!

Everyone at the table should speak of their gratitude for the gifts of the season, the riches of the harvest, and the many blessings. Storytelling, singing, and dancing should all be a part of this jubilant festival.

Gather Together

Table with chairs

Brightly colored cloth

Flowers in summer colors

Plates and napkins

Goblets

Bottle of wine

Bread knife

Loaf of bread

*Cheese or your choice
of spread*

Dishes of nuts

Corn cobs

Bunch of grapes

Salt

LITHA'S LONGEST DAY: MIDSOMMAR RITE

Sometimes simplicity is the most effective approach for the observation of a high holiday. This Summer Solstice ritual for one is very straightforward. All you need is a spot with a view of the northeastern horizon, a blanket to sit on, and a glass of water. You'll also have to get up very early to catch the rising sun on this, the longest day of the year (June 21). In northern Europe, this major sabbat was called Litha.

Do your due diligence in advance and research the exact moment when the dawn breaks and the sun, our beloved source of heat, light, and life, shows itself. It is usually just a few minutes after 5am. Find a spot where you'll have a view of the northeastern horizon: your backyard, a city park, or some other outdoor spot where you'll be mostly undisturbed. Your spot doesn't have to be perfect—you just need to be able to see the sun shortly after it rises over the hills, trees, and houses.

Grab your blanket and water a few minutes before dawn. Move to your ritual spot. Stand facing East and say:

I come to this place and this time to celebrate the Summer Solstice.

Each point of the compass corresponds with one of the different elements. So, as you invoke each point of the compass and its associated elemental energy, dip your fingers in the water in your glass and fling it in that direction:

N

Face North and say:

Spirits of the North, Spirits of Earth, I call to you. Come into this circle, I ask, and share your stability. On this, the longest day, welcome Earth!

W

Face West and say:

Spirits of the West, Spirits of Water, I call to you. Come into this circle, I ask, and share your love. On this, the longest day, welcome Water!

YOU

E

Face East and say:

Spirits of the East, Spirits of Air, I call to you. Come into this circle, I ask, and share your wisdom. On this, the longest day, welcome Air!

Face South and say:

Spirits of the South, Spirits of Fire, I call to you. Come into this circle, I ask, and share your inspiration. On this, the longest day, welcome Fire!

S

Once you have called upon the spirits, stand and feel the sun upon your face and skin. Sit down and meditate, reflecting on what you envision for this golden summer season, and stay as long as you wish. When you are ready, fold up the blanket and pour the remaining water into the earth as an offering. As you return home, think about how lucky we are to be living on this beautiful planet and what you can do to protect and give back to Mother Earth.

The Nordic Calendar: A Lunar System

The early folk of Scandinavia, including the Vikings, did not have four seasons as we do today. Instead, they only had two seasons: summer and winter. The year was not divided into months, as most countries do today in accordance with the Gregorian calendar, which was introduced in October 1582 by Pope Gregory XIII. Instead, the Vikings followed a lunar calendar that counted from new moon to new moon or full moon to full moon. The word "month" is still referred to as the moon in Scandinavia—in Danish, for example, it is called *måned*, which is derived from a word meaning both "month" and "moon."

As you will see from the names of the various months, the Vikings were mainly farmers who were very dependent on the seasons and the weather. The lunar-based calendar changes each year, as do all moon-based systems.

Winter Months

Gormánuður: The first winter month is called butcher month, and a feast called Winter Blót is held on the first day of this month (a *blót* is a ceremonial offering). This feast is to honor Freya in gratitude for the harvest.

Ýlir: The second winter month is called Yule month, which is derived from one of Odin's many names: Jólnir (from the word *jól*). During this time, Odin travels around Midgard and children fill socks with hay for his horse Sleipnir. The god might give them a small gift in return. The Yule month is also connected with fertility and planning to grow the crops.

Mörsugur: The third winter month is associated with the word fat, referring to animal and bird fat. Some call this the "Bone-Marrow Sucking" month. It is the month when the Winter Solstice is held, which usually falls on December 21.

Þorri: The fourth winter month is called Þorri, which is sometimes referred to as Thorri, a beloved winter spirit. This is the month when the feast of Torrablot is held. The night before this month begins, the woman of the house will walk outside and welcome Thorri inside as a guest. This is still celebrated in Iceland every year.

Gói: The fifth winter month is associated with the daughter of Thorri. In older times, villages would hold a Gói *blót* in this month. It is also known as women's month.

Einmánuður: Now comes the harbinger of spring, and the vernal equinox is celebrated during this time. The sixth and last winter month is dedicated to boys.

Summer Months

Harpa: This is the first summer month and was when the third largest *blót*, called the Summer Blót, would be held. This is largely a feast in honor of the god of war, Odin. The name Harpa is feminine—in fact, this is also the month for celebrating girls. Harpa is still recognized in Iceland today.

Skerpla: This is the second summer month. A female name, Skerpla is believed to refer to a time of growth. The woman goddess for whom this month was named has passed out of history.

Sólmánuður: The third summer month is known as the "sun month," and it is the brightest time of the year in Scandinavia. The Summer Solstice, which mostly falls on June 21, is also held in this month.

Heyannir: The fourth summer month is called Heyannir or "haymaking," which is the month for drying and harvesting hay and the joyous time when reaping can begin.

Tvímánuður: The last summer month is called corn-cutting month. This is the time to harvest fruits and plant bulbs for the first blooms of the coming transition from winter to spring.

Haustmánuður: The last summer month is called harvest month. This is a time to bless all the farmers and folks who make sure everyone is fed In the winter season.

COLD MOON RISING WINTER SOLSTICE RITUAL

Gather Together

Outdoor or indoor altar

Small cauldron with a handle

Large pillar candle

Stems of mistletoe and ivy

Branches of holly, pine, cedar, and juniper

Matches

Beer, mulled wine, hot apple cider, and/or mead

Selection of warm festive foods

Winter Solstice rituals (on December 21) traditionally celebrate the rebirth of the sun, which is especially vital in colder climes. Time spent together with loved ones by the roaring heat of a fire should be regarded as deeply sacred.

Gather outside or near a homely hearth. Place the cauldron with the candle inside on the altar and surround it with stems of mistletoe and ivy, as well as branches of holly, pine, cedar, and juniper. The participants should also wear crowns woven from mistletoe and ivy. Begin the ritual by holding hands around the fire. Hum softly and gradually build the hum to a shout. This represents the cries of the goddess giving birth once again to the sun and a new year. The ritual leader says:

All bow to the East!

Hail to the newborn Sun,

And to the Great Goddess who has brought him forth!

Everyone now bows to honor the Sun God and the Mother Goddess. The ritual leader then chants:

Freya, Holda, Brigid, Cerridwen, Heaven's Queen,

By the light of this moon in this dark night,

Teach us the mystery of rebirth.

The ritual leader lights the candle in the cauldron while everyone thinks of the new year to come. Now is the time when the Goddess will reveal herself privately to each participant. Even if you are indoors by the fire, the Goddess will still make herself known in your heart. Now the ritual leader says:

Queen of the Stars,

Queen of the Moon,

Queen of the Earth,

Bringer of Fire,

Giver of Life,

*The Great Mother gives birth
to this new year,*

And we are her witnesses.

And so mote it be!

Everyone then shouts:

Blessed be!

A toast to the new sun should take place with beer, mulled wine, hot apple cider, or mead and a selection of warm festive foods.

LUCKY WITCH'S MOON: FRIDAY THE THIRTEENTH

We honor Freya every week, but also in a very special way a few times a year when there is a Friday the 13th. This is for two reasons. Firstly, the English word Friday comes from the Scandinavian name for this day of the week, Frjádagr, and so Friday is "Freya's Day." Secondly, Freya's special number is 13, and therefore any Friday the 13th is also her day and a time to celebrate this great, witchy goddess.

Ancient Astrology for Modern Pagans

Aries: March 21–April 19

As a cardinal fire sign, and the first of the 12 signs of the zodiac, the Aries' idea of a good time usually involves a bonfire. Characterized by having a strong will, the Aries ram drives forward without looking from side to side. Even if this is not your sun sign, you can still honor your inner fire with the color red and the driving force of Aries—although it may get you into trouble!

Aries roles: Fire dancer, chef, warrior, glassblower, entrepreneur

Taurus: April 20–May 20

The fixed earth sign of Taurus, symbolized by the mighty bull, will not tolerate lies, dishonor, or false pledges. Characterized as the gravity-wielding earth goddess of all, the healing Taurus will be seen growing and gathering wild herbs to brew a healing tea, so it is best to join forces with her to save the planet for our future and that of all who come after us.

Taurus roles: Witch, magical gardener, herbalist, medicine woman, healer

Gemini: May 21–June 20

The star sign represented by twins is the air sign to outwit all air signs. Brilliant and original thinkers, the intuitive and poetic Gemini will "out-prose" everyone—they can explain anything to anyone. Their love of learning is limitless!

Gemini roles: Educator/advocate, poet, writer, alchemist, public speaker

Cancer: June 21–July 22

Cancer, ruled by the beloved moon, is linked to all things lunar, including cats, night-time magic, moods, brews, and much more. These sensitive folk are also very psychic and make for good tarot readers as well as healers.

Cancer roles: Tarot reader, cook, vintner, jeweler, interior decorator

Leo: July 23–August 22

A fire sign symbolized by the mighty lion, Leo is inspiring and has a huge heart. The loveable show-off, Leo, wants to paint, sing, and dance. Leo can bring out the life of any party in grand style.

Leo roles: Musician, actor, painter, CEO, filmmaker, priestess

Virgo: August 23–September 22

Beloved Virgo, an earth sign, remains rational and has the ability to analyze and make sense of everything. These logical lovelies are also gifted doctors and nurses. Truth be told, Virgoans can do anything to which they put their very smart minds. Virgoans are also very sensitive and beautifully humble about this attribute.

Virgo roles: Writer, psychiatrist, physician, herbal header, dietician, cook, teacher

Libra: September 23–October 22

Represented by a set of scales, Librans are known for having a strong desire to create harmony and balance. They love to find the balance between the sacred and the everyday, the dark and the light. Ruled by Venus, the goddess of love, Librans are also romantic souls, so they love performing a love spell or two.

Libra roles: Playwright, performer, designer, artist, couple's counselor, attorney, editor

Scorpio: October 23–November 21

Scorpios are fixed water signs who are represented by the scorpion, whose sting is there to protect. Uncover your innermost Scorpio self with a solo spiritual journey to a place that really challenges you. Of all the signs, Scorpios have the potential to soar the highest (although the opposite is true as well). However, following your inner guidance will get you to the top.

Scorpio roles: Alchemist, scientist, detective, brewer, artist, costumer, perfumer

Sagittarius: November 22–December 21

Brazen, forward-thinking, and fiery, Sagittarius is characterized by a half-man/half-beast character, shooting its arrow into the sky. Never one to look back and linger for too long, Sagittarius moves forward with a definitive swiftness that can sometimes be so rapid it is not even seen. Quick-witted and self-assured, the archer charges forward in the most positive way.

Sagittarius roles: Executive, printmaker, software designer, engineer, art director, vet

Capricorn: December 22–January 20

Characterized as the mountain goat, the Capricorn has an honest disposition and is ready for action and success, all backed up with a fantastically artistic side. Nothing can really get in the goat's way, and they are truly loyal to loved ones, friends, and coworkers. They believe in slowly, but surely, climbing the mountaintop to attain all good things, including a great life!

Capricorn roles: Chief executive, manager, impresario, gallerist, actor, financier, landowner

Aquarius: January 21–February 19

Aquarius can be the sign of true genius. Given to flashes of brilliant insight, Aquarius not only has your number, but she accurately dreamed of it three days before you even met her. Aquarians are wonderfully unpredictable and have much to learn as well as much to teach.

Aquarius roles: Composer, guru, inventor, rocket scientist, ceremonialist, shaman, writer

Pisces: February 20–March 20

The star sign represented by the fish is a witch's best friend; they are psychic, sensitive, and offer a lot of love to those in their lives. This sign is both simple and complicated—they are mutable and very chameleon-like, and they excel at whatever they need to do in the moment. The Pisces soul can go deeper than anyone else's. Music can set the mood for Pisceans for meditation and contemplation of the meaning of it all.

Pisces roles: Creative director, dancer, jewelry designer, distiller, candlemaker, ritualist

CONCLUSION: Living a Charmed Life Each and Every Day

Our system of weeks comes to us from our Norse elders of long ago. It is beautifully simple and works wonderfully well. Every day has its own energy, which corresponds to the deities who hold domain over that day. Each day also has its own rhythm as well as personal associations and what we bring to each sunrise. The way we mark and manage our weeks and days is how we spend our lives, so I ask you to approach them mindfully. As a result, you will enjoy each day much more and find that your life has more meaning and magic.

Sunday: Our northern forefolk worshiped the sun because of the extremely cold climate in which they lived. For this reason, they gave the sun its own day and so the first day of the week is called Sunday. On many carvings, rune stones, and tokens, archeologists and historians have found depictions of the sun. These are called *solhjul*, which means "sun wheel." Start your week with a ritual honoring the life-giving sun. It can be as simple as lighting a bright and happy, yellow or orange candle at dawn.

Monday: The moon was also important to our ancestors because it helped them keep track of time using the lunar calendar. Like the sun, the moon had its own day: Monday. Today, in Denmark, which is widely known as the happiest country in the world, Monday is called *Mandag*, while in neighboring Germany it is called *Montag* (from the word *Mond*, which also means "moon"). Our moon is the mirror to our sun and represents emotions, moods, and the realm of psychism and dreams. A lunar rite should be performed at night when the moon has risen, and you can delve into your deepest wisdom.

Tuesday: Northern gods rule the second day of the working week, one that's filled with purpose, effort, and high energy. The Norse god Tyr (see page 42) is associated with Tuesday and in the Scandinavian countries, Denmark, Norway, and Sweden, this day is called *Tirsdag*, which means that Tuesday is "Tyr's day." A way to observe the special energy of Tuesdays, which is akin to the boldness of Mars, is to move or walk or take action in some way. A brisk walking meditation would be an excellent way to take charge of your Tuesdays.

Wednesday: I sometimes refer to Wednesday as Woden's Day, which is yet another way to speak of the chief god of Asgard, Odin, the great king and ruler. The word Woden is derived from the Germanic word *Wotan*, which means "Odin," so Wednesday is "Odin's Day." This is a day of leadership, hunting down your pursuits, and attacking life with full force. Greet your Wednesdays by boosting your self-esteem and fully giving yourself the reigns in your life. Try a meditation focused on boosting your energy to honor yourself.

Thursday: Thor is associated with Thursday, which comes from the word *Torsdag* in the Scandinavian countries. In the Germanic countries, Thursday is called *Donnerstag*, which means "thunder day." This originates from the word *Donar*, which was the Germanic name for "Thor." Thurdays are associated with prosperity, abundance, luck, and positive power. This is an excellent day for a money energy spell using green candles, crystals, and tree magic.

Friday: Friday is named after *Frjádagr* (Freya's Day), one of the festivity days of the week that was sacred to Freya, the greatest goddess of Norse mythology who is also a witch deity. Freya is a protector of all women and girls, and as a goddess guardian holds great power. This is a delightful time to get together with girlfriends to celebrate each other and honor the sanctity of sacred female bonds.

Saturday: Interestingly, the northern tribes held onto the Roman origins of Saturn's Day, and it has lasted ever since. Saturn was the Roman god of agriculture. Although Saturn may sound like a hard taskmaster, the ancients would honor Saturn's Day with feasts since this god held domain over agriculture and, ultimately, planting and harvest. A good way to spend Saturday is with a sacred practice such as planting and tending flowers, herbs, or trees, as this befits the energy of the day, both for the ancients and us today!

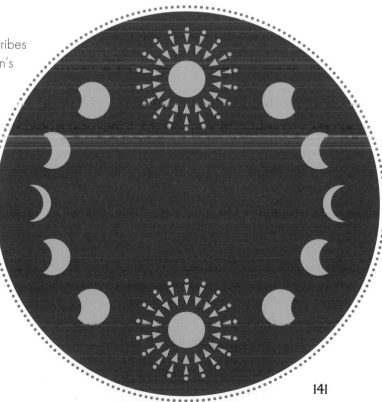

Index

Acknowledgments

I am always grateful to CICO and appreciate their collective high levels of skill and ability to craft lovely books, but I am profoundly moved by the grace and generosity shown to me for this book. Like many folks in the past three years, I have experienced the loss of more than one loved one and also faced health challenges. My two editors, Kristine Pidkameny and Carmel Edmonds, were my rocks who managed to work around my issues. There was never a complaint or a grumble, just more excellence, creativity, unending smarts, and problem solving. This is so rare and for this, I have a heart full of gratitude. My thankfulness extends to the copy-editor Caroline West, who doesn't miss a trick and seems to have encyclopedic knowledge of all things! The designer Emily Breen and illustrator Nina Hunter made magic and every single page is gorgeous. Big thanks to publisher Cindy Richards for having a hugely talented team who is dedicated to beautiful and inspiring books. Brava and thank you.